All Age Worship

MAGGIE DURRAN

D1784492

All Age Worship

MAGGIE DURRAN

Angel Press

First published by Angel Press

©Maggie Durran 1987

All rights reserved.
No part of this publication may be reproduced or transmitted
in any form or by any means, electronic or mechanical, including
photocopying, recording, or any information storage and
retrieval system, without permission in writing from the
publisher.

British Library Cataloguing in Publication Data

Durran, Maggie
  All age worship.
  1. Worship
  I. Title
  264   BV10.2

ISBN 0-947785-17-5

Cover photograph courtesy of Graham Whistler and members
of St. Anne's Church, East Wittering.

All scripts are copyright Maggie Durran, except for the
following:

The Third Little Piggy, copyright Alex Simons and used by
permission.

*The Most Precious Pearl, Come Go With Me to That Land,
God is Our Father, On Tiptoe Dance, Mr. Noah, God is Our
Father Dance,* and *El Shaddai Lord's Prayer Actions,* are
copyright Celebration, PO Box 309, Aliquippa, PA 15001,
USA, All rights reserved, Dance and Action illustrations are
by Ruth Wieting, © Celebration and are used by permission.
Exerpts from the ASB are used by permission of the Central
Board of Finance of the Church of England.
Quotations from the Revised Standard Version of the Bible
are by courtesy of the Division of Education and ministry
of the National Council of the Churches of Christ in the USA.

Photoset in Times by
Woodfield Graphics, Fontwell, West Sussex.

Contents

	Introduction	
1.	Worship and Nurture of Children in the Church	1
2.	The Worship Life of the Church	11
3.	Call to Worship	16
4.	Music	19
5.	The Word of God: Readings	24
6.	Bible Stories: Drama	31
7.	Bible Stories: with Puppets	50
8.	Sermons: Interpreting the Word of God	58
9.	Prayer	73
10.	Dance	75
11.	Symbol and Movement	85
12.	Liturgy	89
13.	Atmosphere and Surroundings	95
14.	Planning and Preparation	99
15.	Discipline	103
16.	All Age Worship and the Eucharist	107
17.	Festivals	112
18.	Workshop Preparation	130
	References and Reading List	136
	Index of Scripts	137

Introduction

All Age Worship has grown out of work in my local church and experience of leading worship and teaching on the theme of All Age Worship at churches and conferences in Britain over the last ten years.

In the busy life of any church, it is always useful to have a source book of resources for worship that can be used as they are or that will trigger the imagination for new material to be devised.

In all age worship and family worship, many churches try to include leaders other than the clergy, training them through the experience of leading. All Age Worship includes both relevant principles and their practical outworking to help all worship leaders develop their skills and understanding as they lead.

Inclusive forms have been used throughout; masculine and feminine forms of pronouns are used when relating to a person in the singular, as with child or leader. This avoids any suggestion that the person in question is necessarily male. God is referred to by the masculine pronoun; though unquestionably beyond our categories of human gender, there is no generally acceptable alternative pronoun.

In all quotations the Revised Standard Version of the Bible is used

People experience God's presence in the world and in all creation, where God is revealed and is perceived with the senses as well as the mind, in daily experience as well as in the truth of Scripture. In Ezekiel Chapter 36:24-28, the words hold promise of a living relationship with God in 'the heart of flesh' and of a renewed ability to live faithfully each day, not because the laws are well memorised but because of the indwelling spirit which enables the people to live according to God's ordinance.

God is constantly revealing himself to all people through life, experience, circumstances and relationships. Such revelation is not always acknowledged; people are not necessarily aware of God's presence. It is as if they have not been introduced to him. Sometimes they have been taught falsely and the signs of God's presence are seen as coincidence. Contemporary ideas and prejudices in society also can stop people recognising God in their experience.

Experiences that are perceived as more intuitive or emotional are just as real as the scientific or the reasoned. Recent centuries have seen the Church having a decreasing awareness of the 'mysterious' dimension of life in the face of the scientific or reasoned. Yet the mystery of God is perceived or apprehended by the senses as well as the intellect as far as it can be perceived at all.

Relationship to God is built in communion with God - a prayer conversation - in which the person hears God speak as well as speaking to him, with the whole being: mind and emotions. In John 14:15-24 Jesus tells his disciples of the very intimate nature of the relationship between God and those who are his people. The Spirit would come to them and they would also know that Jesus and the Father would make their home with that person. God: Father, Son, and Spirit, would be closer to that person than any other person could ever be, and in this is the peace of which Jesus talked in the later verses of the chapter. This is a particular peace, *Shalom*, which is not an absence of sound in a cessation of all activity and strife, but the active peace of harmony and of all things working together. It reflects the idea of strong, working co-operation between God and the human person, living in communion and working in co-operation.

Prayer is an ongoing communion with God. It involves being conscious of God, through reason in the truth of the Scriptures, through the teaching of the Church, and the history of God's people. It must also involve the inner, intuitive sense of God's presence, the emotional and that which "stirs the heart." Awareness of the dimension of mystery and God's 'otherness' comes in this latter while reason and the truth of scripture give order, stability, and discernment.

Conversation and communion between the Christian and God includes silence, reading, listening, talking. Prayer life can be much enriched by developing those aspects of spirituality that have been less emphasised in the Protestant churches since the Reformation: meditation, contemplation and silence.

What is corporate worship?

Since Old Testament times, God has been creating a body of people who will live according to his purpose. When they come to worship together they are coming to be made into that people, not simply to satisfy individual need or to make a personal response. They could do that alone. The people of God as the Church is the human expression of the life of God in the Trinity.

To be God's people, since they live in a fallen humanity, they need the continuing work of redemption and formation in their gathering together; God is constantly moulding them into his people. This will only happen to them as they gather together in his presence.

The Church has identity given by God, possible because of redemption, and has communion with him in corporate expressions much like those the individual has in her prayer life. They offer God glory for who he is, in responsive worship; hear the word reasoned and logical through preaching, studying, teaching, reading and reflection together. God speaks through the intuitive through prophecy and tongues. God reveals himself and at times directs and corrects his people. Through all their experience of being together with God they are, and are being made into, his people.

When God's people worship him they are offering to God what is due to him. Glory is offered to God for who he is, for what he has done: for creation, redemption, and wholeness. Thanks are offered to God for his Word by which his people are made new creatures, to live as he intended in creation. Because we still live in this human flesh, with its inheritance of sin we need the ongoing revelation of God's Word to live as he intended, a life of *Shalom* with him. Therefore we seek to be formed by and faithful to his word, individually and together.

Revelation

The revelation of himself is essentially God's own business; he chooses how and to whom he will reveal himself. We may pray for a special revelation, even beg for it, but the revelation of God (the Word) always issues from God not from us. We may only point to it, pray and ask for it. In John 1:1-14 the apostle speaks of the encompassing nature of God's revelation in the Word, that has been present from the beginning of time. God is revealed constantly by the life he created: "In him was life, and the life was the light of men. The light shines in the darkness, and the darkness has not overcome it." There was to be a particular revelation of the Word as a person, the Son of Man, who was also Son of God. There are many particular signs and revelations of God seen in the biblical miracles, in the miracles evident in the early church, and today there are still such special revelations. Yet in ordinary ways God is revealed in the church, week after week and day after day, with a constancy that shows that miracles are not normative experiences of God. Any of these may bring an individual to a sudden consciousness of God: the evidence of God in creation; the gift of Jesus Christ; or the presence of God in a contemporary sign.

Conversion is a term most commonly used to describe that time at which an individual experiences a revelation of God such that he is moved to co-operate with God in discipleship. First, he must be old enough to realise his life can be given to live according to the ordination of God; he is not a child. The moment may have the foundation of a well-ordered understanding of God, perhaps from years of church-going, but equally there are many people who have little understanding, except to be aware intuitively that for their lives to be fulfilled something more is needed. The event of such conversion can be like falling in love, an overwhelming sense of the presence of God as love and as all that is good. The evidence of such conversion is that the person's life is changed in its order, its purpose, and its hope. That co-operation with the work, power and grace of God will be seen in the fruit of the Spirit.

In an adult Christian there is the self-discipline of discipleship. This latter is ongoing conversion as the person changes and matures. It is the longing to change which happens in conversion, not a complete life discipline. Each Christian spends his entire life becoming a disciple. An adult relationship with God involves taking responsibility for staying in fellowship, for self-discipline, for acknowledging and confessing the sin that works against wholeness. The adult Christian chooses to continue and keep current his relationship to God.

Revelation, conversion and discipleship are linked together. Without revelation there is no conversion and no discipleship. But as God is revealed in the Church, in the Sacraments and in the Word, children and adults are present. However it is as children mature and are self-disciplined in the various aspects of human life that Christian discipleship is relevant to them.

CHILDREN IN THE CHURCH

In present-day society and in the Church there are many false distinctions between old and young, between secular and religious, between families and individuals. Many of the distinctions are made more significant by an over-emphasis on the individual without a parallel awareness of the God-given meaning of the family, community, and nations, for all human life. The Church is complicit in the fragmentation typical of Western society. Much influenced by the culture around, the Church sees children as essentially different beings and its emphasis on a heady, intellectual religion has reinforced this.

For leaders of churches and those who have responsibility for children, there is much to be re-evaluated, as the same culture has trained us through individualism and consumerism to be alienated, isolated and separated from our neighbours, although the church is essentially a community, reflecting the community of the Trinity.

Many of the difficulties with children are the result of thinking that faith in God is based on understanding, an aspect of the intellect. In fact faith in God is based first on God's action in redemption. We are saved not by our efforts or our thinking but by grace, a free gift of God. Revelation similarly is a gift from God that a child may receive. God's gift is not conditional. We become confused because we have unconsciously learned that the way we are able to behave or to think affects God's redemption.

Maturity in the Christian life is developed through understanding and experience, through discipleship, as we are able to choose to order our lives according to his purpose, and choose to be discipled. Discipleship, which implies taking responsibility for the establishing of the Kingdom on earth, can only happen in people who have a sense of their own life, and the ability to give it to what purpose they will.

There are many people in our churches who, having no sense of themselves as responsible people, cannot yet be discipled. They are like the birds in The Parable of The Mustard Seed. (Matt.13:31-32) They do receive life through the church, they believe in God's love, may see him revealed, but have no power of self-determination in their own lives.

Where a church sees itself to be God's people there will be members in all these states. There are those who are dependent and those who are not. There will be those who are learning to recognise God's presence, those who are following even though they cannot yet see, those who feel loved and love in response but are not yet at an age of responsibility, and there will be those who are responsible and maturing in their discipleship. All are members of God's people, just as in a nation all are members though many are children, old, infirm, or handicapped.

A church living as God's people can sustain collective responsibility for the lives of dependent members, just as a family takes collective responsibility for its children. The faith of dependent members happens in the midst of the church to which they belong. They are nurtured as they are present. Through experience they will become more aware of God and recognise his presence in the world. On reaching an age of decision they will take responsibility for their own lives, choosing discipleship − or not.

A church can create a nurturing environment in which many people may experience God's life while they are yet unable to take full responsibility. Children grow up to where they will take responsibility, so it is the church's task to create the best possible environment for them to experience and recognise God's presence and love, to experience and learn what it is to be God's people. Children should participate as fully as possible in the life of the church for this to happen, for the church is one of those places in the arena of life where God is particularly revealed. The church is a sign of God.

SPIRITUAL DEVELOPMENT OF CHILDREN

Children are received into the church as babies, in a variety of ways that reflect our denominational understandings. For many there is the sacrament of baptism; for others there is a service of dedication. Whichever we have chosen for our children, we are concerned to understand and nurture their faith in God and to develop their relationship to the church as God's people. From the time of conception, a child is a spiritual being.

The person's relationship to God, in which spirituality is expressed, is first a gift from God. St John in his epistle said that we love because he first loved us. In the same epistle, Chapter 2, Verses 12 to 14, John addressed himself to several groups within the church, the little children, the fathers and the young men. To the "little children" he wrote, "because you know the Father." It is for the Church today to grasp what it means for little children to know the Father.

How can the church begin to understand a child's relationship to God, and her spirituality which is the expression of that relationship? How can parents nurture the child's relationship to God and how can the church include children and nurture them in relationship to God.

The child finds her own identity as she is loved, protected and provided for, first by her parents. The appropriate relationship between parent and child is first for them to give and her to receive. This giving is unconditional: the baby receives gratuitously, her response to parents is enjoyed and appreciated but not demanded. She is not rejected when she fails to smile or please her parents, or if she cries when this is inconvenient to them. So too with God. The love of God is expressed to the child through people, the parents, the family, friends and neighbours, and the church. Being loved is an essential foundation to being able to give love in return. All the aspects of affirmation, respect, appreciation, and friendship that are given to a child help towards her own mature adult response to God and to others in later years.

Creation is an expression of God, and reveals his life to a child. The wind, the sun, the clouds and rain, light and dark, are immediate experiences for a child. The richness of her experience introduces the child to the richness of God. A child who has never seen or climbed a mountain or paddled in the sea will have little ability to appreciate them. The child's ever-widening experience through home and school introduces her to greater potential for appreciating the diversity and creativity of God. Whether learning to read, or studying mathematics, a child is uncovering the beauty of the order of created life, both full of pattern and yet open to endless possibilities, like a kaleidoscope. So as a child grows, the richer her experience of God's creation, the greater can be her sense of wonder at the majesty and power of God.

Both the loving relationships and the experience of creation are raw materials of spiritual development, which the child receives and in response to which she can grow to give in return. The many aspects of daily life and of relationships, where love and creation are continuing experiences, enable a child to respond and perceive God as Father and Creator, the one in whom life finds its meaning. These are the spiritual aspects in which the rest of life is contextualised and encompassed.

For a child to respond to God in worship, with her thanks and her service, there are many ways in which parents and other adults may nurture the child, and help her to an expression of faith appropriate to her age and understanding.

Parents and Family

Parents offer a very special committed love to a child. This love is peculiar to their relationship and at the same time expresses particular aspects of God's love to the child. The parents are those who unconditionally cherish and comfort the baby. While others may at times offer expressions of love, in such circumstances their gift is temporary, whereas parents have chosen, in having a child, to give without measure. This is a shadow or reflection of the love that Christ offered to all creation in his act of taking on human form; he expressed the unconditional love of God in the everyday human situation.

Prayers in the Family

In the family, a child begins to glean his first understanding that God is the source of life, of love and of creation, through seeing and hearing the family relationship to God. Family prayers offer thanks to God for the goodness around them. The family prays about the problems of daily work and living so the child is aware of God's concern for the concerns of the family.

For some families, a regular Bible reading and a spontaneous prayer from one of the family is a common form of family prayer. Other families find it more constructive to follow established liturgical forms and use readings set for each day from Bible notes or a lectionary.

There is no merit in setting up an arduous form for daily prayers in the family. Jesus pointed this out to the Pharisees who made hard work out of worship, as if this would earn them credit with God. Rather Jesus suggested that the people should pray simply, and then he taught them the Lord's Prayer.

Church and Family

A worship service is the time when the people of God in a church meet together to worship God and hear him together. Being part of such events is an essential element in the nurture of the child's faith. Among God's people, a child hears of God's goodness, experiences God's Word among his people, finds love and acceptance, joins in worshipping God, and takes part in the people's faithful response to God's call.

For under-threes the primary gifts that the church has are those of belonging to the church and receiving unconditional love. Belonging finds its expression in baptism and participation as a member. The affectionate welcome as a friend, the tolerance, the patient sharing of books, the encouragement to participate, are expressions of the church's love and care for small children. The child's appropriate response to God is to be in the midst, as a recipient of these.

For three to six-year-olds, through the years of playgroup and infant school, a child is beginning to feel a sense of the group and wants to be included in its activity. While a baby is content to have his needs met through a caring adult with personal love and affection, the growing child now wants to be part of the game, the family meal, or social occasion. Though the will is there, the skills may not be.

Recognising the children's wish to participate in the group activity, a church service can be structured and planned with emphasis on the congregation's participation.

Avoid the pitfall of creating a *Children's Service*. Plan all age worship, for then children are nurtured through being among a worshipping people; it does little for them to be the focus of the service, when the stated purpose of a worship event is to focus on God.

This rudimentary sharing in the group, both church and family, is an expression of the child's spirituality at this age. He is a dependent member of the church, having no separate and distinct discipleship of his own. Just as his everyday life is maintained by his parents and family, so his response to God is dependent on others. If those around him do not worship God, the child does not.

Six to twelve-year-olds have mastered many basic skills of language and negotiation. They can read, often quite fluently, can follow instructions, can think out plans and schedules, and are happy to serve others in order to gain a common objective. They often happily curtail their own plans to fit in with other people, but are discouraged if the group does not give them an opportunity to be creative and expressive. This age group thrives more than any other in an inclusive approach to church worship. The child can quickly become distracting and destructive, however, if the church expects him to be present as audience but not participant. Given the chance to participate, he can be wholehearted and generous.

Eight to twelve-year-olds volunteer their help in music, drama, prayers, dance, and as acolytes and stewards. To adults who are more complicated and subtle in response to God, the child's involvement may appear naive. Yet often the child has a faith in God's goodness and love that is remarkably trusting and straightforward. God does hear the prayers of children, so their trust is not ill-founded.

A church that establishes a worship service for all ages, that recognises that worship is by definition essentially an act of participation in an offering to God, can give an immeasurable amount to children of these ages. The church's gift to children is in making a way open for children to give their response to God along with the rest of the congregation. The child will not be satisfied with a *children's slot* in the service, for that implies first that the child is there to receive when really he is nurtured most through giving. Secondly it says that his presence throughout the remainder of the service is not relevant to God.

Those who lead worship for all ages, with a concern for the nurture of all members will then look for structures, forms and liturgies that facilitate the worship of *everyone* present, in an all-age worship service.

The teenager should have the opportunity to discover and assert for himself the foundational direction of his life. He is able to participate as an adult in the life of the church, and able to take responsibility for his own prayer and worship life. The spiritual task of the teenager includes discovering for himself how he is going to take up the responsibility of discipleship and how he is going to follow God's call on his life. Where parents have been responsible for his life and growing knowledge of God, this now becomes the child's own responsibility.

Most churches with active teenage members find their nurture is best served with a youth group in addition to full participation in worship. Teenagers have particular questions and responses to consider, and are helped by having someone with whom they identify and a group to go to in which such questions can easily be asked without embarrassment. Both teenagers who are more committed and those who are "anti-church" can find their help in this group.

As young people begin to take up responsibility for their own lives spiritually, the church should ensure there is room for them to give and serve, taking responsibility in its life. There should be opportunity to be responsible in worship and in the church's caring ministry. Young people who are discovering their own maturity as individuals either find access to being responsible members of the church, or they conclude that the church is empty of meaning in not being a place for their active participation as adults.

EDUCATION AND NURTURE

Nurture is the care and concern for the developing spiritual growth of all the members of the church, within the context of the Church as God's people. To be nurtured in their faith the members of a church must experience God together, both adults and children. The local church is where we see and experience God working now. This awareness, made possible through sharing, testimony and prayer, is essential to the faith of the individual. History teaches how God works, but only our everyday experience of him increases our faith. This awareness and growth comes *only through experience*.

Education is the acquisition of knowledge, and that is equally the pastoral responsibility of the church, as it is also necessary for maturity. The identity and structure of the church is the framework that sets the faith of the individual into the context of the history of God's people. The Bible and Church history show how individuals have experienced God through the ages and how God has directed his people. These are important in giving understanding of the way in which God works. People can learn *about* these.

Children learn through experience; information is retained as they perceive its meaning and relevance in everyday life. In a lecture, John Tomlinson, Chief Education Officer for Cheshire, aptly underlined this saying, 'Practice must take an emotional root before it becomes a rational behaviour.'[1] If the church is concerned for the developing life and discipleship of those who come into the church, old or young, this emotional root of experience is the critical point. The emotional root will determine the future pattern of development. It is of utmost significance, therefore, to determine what it is that children are experiencing and therefore learning.

Children's Experience

Life is an integrated entity that cannot be separated into compartments, like the pound of flesh for Shylock. The Greek concept of a separate and distinct soul to which questions of a spiritual nature could be addressed is unacceptable to biblical understanding and to contemporary doctrine.[2] Experience teaches the whole person. Children learn about life through what they live, interpreting their experience as people around them influence their way of perceiving.

The church wants to be the people of God, a body whose lives are integrated around their individual and corporate faith and in this nurture their children.

During a typical week, the lives of children are ordered by a variety of groups and experiences, all of which help set the way they interpret life: home, television, cinema, church, clubs, organisations such as Scouts, friends, schools, playgroup, Local Council, politicians, shops, advertisers, Social Services. How significant is the church in this list?

There is enormous relevance for this question in the first five years of life, for during this time children are learning and establishing life values. What experience is the church giving the under-five-year-old in terms of the foundations for spiritual development, the meaning of person, the love of God, and the signs of his presence in and around the child. The emotional root will control what is learned. What, in his experience of the church, is being communicated? What is being learned, and how are children learning?

Faith and hope grow through ongoing fellowship in the church. Rich friendships with people who have faith in God will enable children to know God as their Father, assimilating the truth through non-verbal as well as verbal communication.

What are the messages, verbal and non-verbal, that children receive in church ?

When the congregation arrives at church some people are chosen to receive a book and a coloured news-sheet; they are greeted by name and their hand shaken warmly. Others, who come as often, may receive a half smile, a puzzled and quizzical look as the sidesman does not know their names. So children are 'told' that they are not *real* members, do not *really* belong, God is not interested in them.

In the Anglican service the congregation say "in the one spirit we were all baptised into one body." Later the priest reads "We break this bread to share in the body of Christ," with the congregation responding "Though we are many we are one body because we all share in the one bread." Are they aware of the anomaly of saying this with children present, who have been received into membership but may not receive the bread and wine? The anomaly is more common as increasing numbers of churches make a Sunday morning Eucharist the key service in the church's worship life for all ages.

The congregation has declared that through *baptism* they are one body, and that this is realised in the bread shared; but from this only, the high point of the service, the children are excluded. The words and actions are not integrated; something is very wrong with either the words or the actions. There is, as long as this disintegration is present, a clear message to children, for actions speak louder than words. It is time for the Church to integrate its understanding of the sacraments with its liturgy in words and practice.

To use such negative examples is perhaps unfair. However to families with a Christian commitment this matters. If it is our concern that our children experience the spiritual dimension of life from a Christian perspective we will want to determine the quality and type of their experience so that we build what we wish to build.

Many churches are not really happy with the disintegrated path they are following, and are making serious and concerted efforts to integrate the principles concerned (see Chapter Sixteen). There are aspects of contemporary Church life that work against that process of integrating children into the key worship services. Many faithful members come to church in pursuit of their own personal relationship to God, without the recognition of the church as a corporate expression of Christ in a corporate offering to God, with the result that they resent anything that intrudes into or detracts from that individual pursuit. As long as it is implied that the real church is the clergy and professionals,[3] the ordinary members of the congregation will not have a sense of responsibility for the nurture of dependent members and will tend to continue to push that pastoral task onto the clergy and a set of volunteer Sunday School teachers, *without realising that it is what they, the church, do which is the means of nurture.*

The resolution of the theological and theoretical problem is possible, and still church leaders may be deterred from going further in integrating the church's children into worship. The next barrier is how to include them without violation of either the children, the adults, or the encounter with God. To overcome this barrier, *All Age Worship* develops plans and resources for all ages to worship God together.

For Children?

Leaders often think of their work with children as a task for children's sake, because the child has much to learn as she grows up in the church. The latter is undoubtedly true as children need education, knowledge and understanding. But when we consider nurture, then all of us need to grow in faith, and in this sense it is the quality of life which we all have together that is critical and to which children contribute with the adults, all together becoming God's people. In Mark 10:13-16 we read:

> They brought children for him to touch. The disciples rebuked them, but when Jesus saw this he was indignant, and said to them, "Let the children come to me; do not try to stop them; for the Kingdom of God belongs to such as these. I tell you whoever does not accept the Kingdom of God like a child will never enter it." And he put his arms round them, laid his hands upon them, and blessed them.

What is it about children that Jesus would say to us through this passage today? Not that children are especially holy. Perhaps that they are open and trusting in their approach to life. But essentially that it is the nature of the body of Christ that children are included. Matthew 18:1-14 addresses the same issue.

A Christian church, as a nurturing community, must accept a two-way process with children and adults learning together and from one another and growing alongside one another. Where a church is a nurturing community it will begin to recognise the word and work of God in all the members.

A church nurtures children in the Christian life through the qualities of the Christian group: reverence for God and Creation, and caring for each other, primarily the *way* in which the church does what it does. It is being present to the church's faith and worship that gives children an experience in which they can begin to recognise God's warmth, God's love and his hope.

Notes

1. John Tomlinson at the National Children's Bureau, 18th February 1982, and subsequently in *Parenting Papers 2*, from the National Children's Bureau.
2. *Faith in the City*, para. 3.10.
3. *A Strategy for the Church's Ministry* by John Tiller, CIO Publishing, 1983.

CHAPTER TWO: The Worship Life of the Church

All age worship is set in the context of a worshipping people. In life and in worship, the people of God are aware of their relationship to God, Father, Son and Holy Spirit, and that relationship is lived out with fellow members of the church. The primary relationship of church members is of being sisters and brothers in a family of God's people. Within that relationship some people are leaders and elders responsible for the nurture of each member and of the corporate life of the church.

The worship service is a gathering of the whole church to worship together. It is not just a children's service, nor an adult service in which children are onlookers. Worship is for the whole congregation, old, young, single, married, adult, and child. It is necessary to see all members as one group, while being conscious of the diversity of people.

Coming together as a congregation for worship means that each person experiences appropriate participation and expression in worship to God. Also it means the church is growing into a meaningful corporate expression in relation to God. An all age worship service does not need to cater to a succession of interest groups: old, young, teens, nuclear families, single people, vicar, organist, choir. Each of these has their personal interests and preferences but the service is not set around consecutively giving each of them what they want, but discovering the form in which they can worship as one, giving themselves to God.

Work, worship, and celebration are the corporate inter-generational activities of a community of people whose life is focussed on God. These three belong to the family and to all the members; these are what the church does together and it is in them that the spiritual nature of the church is apparent. Life that follows the pattern established by God in creation contains those three elements in balance with each other so a church or community living a corporate redeemed life will hold those three elements in careful balance.

THE ORDER OF WORSHIP

The individual's spiritual life is essential to discipleship and is nurtured in the person's own prayer life. The church's worship life is the structure by means of which the people give themselves to God, as a people. The worship structure is built around several factors.

Worship happens with **regularity** in being together before God when the whole church can be present, on Sunday.

Worship is **orderly**. Being together for the activity of worship requires an order and manner that enables the whole congregation to offer themselves and respond to God.

Worship is **seasonal**. Most older Christian traditions have included a seasonal approach that offers a very broad basis for the church's life. Lent is a time of repentance and fasting; Advent is a time of preparation for Christ's coming. These seasons may not relate to particular individual 'struggles' but will provide for the undergirding of the corporate faith. Such seasons are not necessarily recognised with the same importance today, as the culture of Western society is highly individualistic and has a lower value on what is not necessarily measured by the individual's feeling. We have to recollect the corporate identity as God's people to realise the seasons and how they relate to worship, for repentance and fasting, for festivity and thanksgiving.

Worship includes **wholeness**, being presented by integrated people. As discipleship and faith are integrated into daily life so people bring their whole life as an offering in worship. The activity of worship must therefore be recognised as verbal and nonverbal, logical and reasoned, ecstatic, emotional, intuitive, repetitive, surprising, adventurous, and humourous. In the story of the Israelites leaving Egypt and in the stories of Ezra and Nehemiah are exciting examples of life and worship being integrated and expressing the whole person.

Integrating the Word and Daily Life

Contemporary educational study, as in the work of Paulo Freire, shows us that growth comes from a particular series of steps.[1] Stage one is action, conscious or habitual or imposed. It includes the patterns of everyday existence. Stage two is reflection, conscious consideration of the action, its effects, its meaning, and possible change. Stage three is renewed action, by conscious choice; this is followed by further reflection as in Stage One. The processes of adult learning are also explained fully in Anton Baumohl's *Making Adult Disciples*.[2]

Through such a process, people are enabled to take charge of and direct their own life. The model of action, real reflection and renewed action helps the church understand the processes necessary for them to consider their own action in the light of God's word and to change their patterns of life to accommodate more fully the gospel principles. Thus, the teaching life of the local church has the undergirding principle of being relevant to the ordinary, everyday life of the people, and has to be seen by them to be relevant.

The worship life of God's people involves both real action in the way they live out their calling and symbolic action in liturgy. It is by the process of the people reflecting on both of these, and in being enabled to integrate them, that the work of becoming God's people is accomplished.

When children are in the midst of this process, they experience the symbolic action in services and see the everyday life, so they assimilate the meaning and relevance of faith to life. As the church together reflects on those actions, patterns and perspectives become apparent. These enable everyone to make a fuller, more conscious and far reaching response to day-to-day experience of God.

The worship structure also includes concern for aspects of personal need. Unless given room in the life of the church to express what is personal, it can be very hard for the individual to recognise that God is concerned for her personally. The nurture of the individual child in her faith is relatively little understood in individual families, especially for those who are new to the faith. The service usually then involves elements of both personal faith and growth as well as the corporate already mentioned.

Tempted both by the apparent breakdown of family life and of local community life, and by individualism, the church has, in trying to meet the individual need, often lost sight of the corporate. To live as God's people it is necessary to have corporate worship, family worship and individual worship. As the church fails to see these needs there is confusion that worship leaders struggle to overcome. Is the sermon a sharing of God's word to the people of God together and reflection on their offering to him? Is the sermon there first to 'feed the individual'? The service will feed the individual but the congregation comes into God's presence together primarily to give God what is due to him, not to get what they want.

LEADING GOD'S PEOPLE IN WORSHIP

In the church, all members should give and receive, for this brings growth in members and in the church. This is true in all the aspects of the life of God's people and never more so than in worship. It is as God's people gather for a worship service that they choose to be in his presence together as a people, ready to hear him speak to them together, ready to offer him all that he is worthy to receive, to give him glory, honour and faithfulness.

For a people to move as one people, as the Israelites left Egypt for the Promised Land, requires that all be involved actively. In the story of the rebuilding of the City of Jerusalem and of the temple, in Ezra and Nehemiah, there are several references to individuals hearing God tell them to join the effort, according to their gifts. There was a gradual ordering of the life of all the people to the work, to the lifestyle God wanted them to have, and to the order of worship that historically had previously been the pattern for the people of Israel.

Similarly, God has an interest in a relationship to each local church, so worship services have the potential to be not just a form, nor a conglomerate to meet personal needs, but the context in which there is the kind of exchange with God through which he makes for himself a people.

WORSHIP LEADERS

Worship is not something that one person does for all the others or even that a few can do. Those who lead have the responsibility for enabling, structuring and ordering a time for the people to have a creative communion with God, to be consciously in his presence together.

The elements of worship should be planned on the basis that all may participate. This does not mean reducing worship to the lowest common denominator, but having a service that is broad enough for all to be significantly involved.

The worship will also be formed with awareness of a people offering the whole of themselves, not just mind or 'spiritual' compartments, but the whole human being, intuitive and imagining as well as ordered, emotional as well as rational. Participation is with the whole person.

Those who serve as worship leaders among a congregation recognise the partnership in worship between the worship leader and the people. This partnership works in several aspects: the leader is at times speaking on behalf of the group, is facilitating the group expression in worship, and in all age worship is in partnership with other responsible members to draw the dependent members into the worship.

Leaders recognise that the service is a corporate meeting to praise God and consciously to be in his presence together.

Each gathering to worship is unique as an event, yet it takes place in the context of the history of the Church, and leaders should have some awareness of how God through the Holy Spirit has led the Church through history and what the Spirit is doing with the Church today. What is happening to churches around the world; what change, and what ministry is the Spirit leading churches into nationally, and in what overall direction is the Spirit leading this particular church?

The worship leaders should have some apprehension of the Word of God in several dimensions. The Word is spoken in the Scriptures, in teaching, preaching, and prophecy. The Word made flesh is given for the people of God in bread of the Eucharist. The Word is also reflected in the church as the body of Christ.

It is of no use to a congregation if their worship leaders are not prepared to listen to and learn from others. As time passes and as the congregation changes and develops, as the world and the neighbourhood of the church progresses, the worship form and content change. Worship leaders who listen to all that goes on around them will be aware of these changes and can adapt to them. Music leaders can be aware of new music in the church, how that relates to music in contemporary society, and of the form and function of music in the history of the church. The music leader will also listen to visitors to the church who may bring with new understanding of music in worship or bring new songs and hymns. Music leaders represent only one aspect of worship leadership, alongside liturgists, pastoral leaders and teachers who will also be listeners in this way.

Worship leaders are in charge of themselves and are not people who give in to their own interests and feelings during a service. They are able to maintain an awareness of God, the people, and the flow of the service, without being distracted by limited concentration, a wandering mind or stray feelings.

Worship leaders do not have a personal compulsion to control or manipulate worship for their own satisfaction or affirmation. In other words, they do not have an emotional need to have the status of leader; they are freely serving without an investment in continuing in the role if change is helpful to the worship.

Worship leaders should have a gift for facilitating corporate worship and drawing others into leadership where relevant. There are many gifted people in every congregation, and it is the work of worship leaders—who work for the spiritual health and maturity of the church—to encourage those God-given gifts to be offered in worship and in worship leadership.

Worship leaders know the importance of this service to the church and know they have the authority to resist pressure from irrelevant sources.

Those who preside in worship, as well as those who assist, should know the focus and direction of the service. The leaders should have some idea of how to deal with intrusions of the distracting kind, or when the Spirit wishes to intrude into the planned event. Entirely unexpected intrusions, should be handled without panic or fuss. The close working together of the leadership will help this. For example, if someone is taken ill, the president at the service should not be the one to deal directly with the situation, but keep himself or herself concerned for the whole congregation — to give continuity - while someone else cares for the sick person. Thus the flow of worship may continue. The worship leader may recognise the effect of an intrusion and reflect that in the service; when a small child falls from the pew and cries loudly, the leader may lead a prayer for the child at that moment, as everyone present will be wondering about the child's bump and will be very distracted by their concern.

Leaders should jointly reflect on the service, considering how the time went, how the worship flowed, the elements that were disjointed, their own skill in leadership and how improvements might be made. Leaders should also listen for the responses of members of the congregation, for everything from whether everyone could hear sufficiently clearly, to ideas from adults on how children could be more effectively drawn into worship. This humility is necessary to all forms of leadership.

Worship leaders should be confident to address God and all members of the congregation. When serving others, whether with the chalice or other forms of stewardship, the leader should be comfortably able to look everyone in the eye and greet them genuinely and warmly in the name of the Lord. If there are conflicts or resentments between leaders and members of the congregation, worship will not flow easily, particularly if one of the 'feuding' members has a leading role in the service. Conflict cannot always be quickly sorted out, so those leading should be able to express their love and fellowship with one another with integrity, while acknowledging any temporary disagreement.

Whatever one's particular gift in worship leadership, the leader should recognise the place and value of music and other folk arts, gifts of the Spirit and skills of worship leaders.

Notes

1. *Pedagogy of the Oppressed* by Paulo Freire, Seabury.
2. *Making Adult Disciples*, by Anton Baumohl, Scripture Union, 1984.

CHAPTER THREE: Call to Worship

A worship service is a very profound expression of the relationship between God and his people in which all the people are participants. For that experience to be meaningful, the way in which the service opens is of great significance. The traditional liturgies of the church include expressions that facilitate the opening of worship, and even in the most informal service one finds some form of welcome and call to worship is offered. Yet the opening may still fail to fulfil a call to worship for the people, normally because the minister has been unaware of the significance of this opening.

John's first epistle (I John 1:1-4) begins with a statement explaining the purpose of the letter. John and the other disciples had seen and touched the Christ, and now John testifies to their experience, saying "that which we have seen and heard we proclaim to you, so that you may have fellowship with us; and our fellowship is with the Father and with his Son Jesus Christ." Christians are primarily inviting others into their fellowship with God, and any sense of welcoming others among them is to bring them into "our fellowship with the Father and with his Son...." When the congregation and leaders welcome one another at a service of worship they are communicating that they welcome each person during a time in which they are going to meet with the Father. The focus is not on meeting with one another but meeting with God.

In gathering as a body of people to praise and worship the church is entering, for the time of the service, another dimension than that of everyday life. God is timeless, he is outside the limitations of human existence. He is so entirely different that we cannot conceive his nature, because all our conceptions and glimpses are couched in the terms of our mortal existence. All that we know was created by God and through this we begin to know him, and yet must acknowledge he is entirely beyond our imagining. So when we enter a time of worship in which we meet with God, we enter a dimension that is essentially beyond our definition and our control. We are acknowledging and giving ourselves to God, which is to open ourselves to a dimension that is entirely different from ordinary daily existence.

During this time that is entirely other than our ordinary daily existence, we choose to enter into a consciousness of God, aware of his presence, as Creator, as the Alpha and Omega. Having deliberately set aside our cares and concerns, we concentrate on God. This can be paralleled to our choice to give our whole attention to another human being among our families or with friends. Whether or not we are poor at concentrating, and we all have limits to our ability to concentrate, we choose to focus our minds, our emotions, our whole being on God, and as we find ourselves distracted or our minds wandering during the service, we again choose to look to God.

Worship takes us out of ourselves and we give ourselves wholly and without limitation. It is in this sense that marriage is like our relationship to God. Love is self-giving and self-sacrificing and those who enter into that relationship are immensely vulnerable. However to enter this relationship is the beginning of Christian discipleship, for at this moment we open ourselves to the one who will lead and guide. In giving ourselves in love we may enter into that relationship which Jesus intimated (John 5:19,20) when he stated that he did what he saw the Father doing. When we stop all our activity and focus on the Father we may see what he is doing and then may choose as Jesus did.

Calling to worship

The minister may first welcome those present in an acknowledgement of their fellowship with one another. Then she or he draws the attention of the congregation to the intended focus of the service in acknowledging the occasion, the content, and the focus of the time that is to be spent.

How can this opening of the service be led by the minister?

The call to worship is a quiet declaration of our focus, on our intention to offer praise, and our intention to listen. When this purpose is expressed through the words of a minister alone, it should not be presented as an attempt to convince those present of some truth. That would be patronising, for the congregation know they have come for these purposes. But it is a time when a task is undertaken on behalf of the gathering. Like setting the table before a meal and telling others that the meal is ready, even saying grace when everyone is gathered. These expressions are not the meal, but are necessary for the meal to happen.

The opening moments of the service can help the people to set aside the anxious concerns of the day or the week and prepare themselves to concentrate on God. For most congregations, it is helpful to have at least one spoken sentence for this preparation; and that sentence may be followed with a brief silence. The laying aside of everyday concerns is a prelude to acknowledging together the purpose of this gathering of people.

A Bible verse and a time of silence are perhaps the simplest form of a call to worship and are effective for a group that is accustomed to the process of gathering and of beginning to focus themselves before the service begins. However, the more busy the people are in their everyday lives and if they have normally not previously prepared themselves, more time is necessary for this preparation together. Using a corporate prayer can be the most effective inclusive form.

The beginning of the Eucharist has a more lengthy preparation for this purpose, which expresses all this purpose and direction:

> Almighty God,
> to whom all hearts are open,
> all desires known,
> and from whom no secrets are hidden:
> cleanse the thoughts of our hearts
> by the inspiration of your Holy Spirit,
> that we may perfectly love you,
> and worthily magnify your holy name;
> through Christ our Lord. Amen.

This preparatory step, which may be expressed in other forms than the *Collect for Purity*, is essential for a full corporate expression in worship. A group that gathers and hopes to offer themselves to God cannot bypass this preparation, for without it people's minds and bodies are not corporately gathered; there is no common point of entering into that other dimension or of together choosing self-giving love. This step may be expressed informally or in a liturgical form but it is essential to the worship service.

A poem, reading or mime may be used as a part of the call to worship, introducing the theme of the service alongside the other elements of preparation.

Notices

Some churches present their notices at the beginning of the service and this does draw people's minds into a common focus, though it may not be the best for remembering the content at home later. Notices ought not to be placed within the service itself, while if they are at the end they can easily prove an anti-climax. A sheet of notices is best with some verbal acknowledgement of them before the service.

Before the opening sentences of the call to worship is the appropriate time for any notices or information about the shape and flow of the service. Such information can be very intrusive if presented during the service and prior information can mean that only a phrase of reminder is necessary as the service proceeds. Above all, a worship service should flow; it may be rich with movement and a variety of directions but these should flow out of each other, not jerk and bump.

THE PARABLE OF THE LAMP

Mime with reading, based on Luke 8:16-17

Characters: Reader, Lamplighter

Props: lampstand, lamp or large candle, cover for lamp (this can be a tall cylinder of black paper that will go over candle but leaves an opening at the top, to prevent fire or the candle being extinguished.)

The lampstand is placed off-centre of the playing area, but visible to the whole congregation. The place should allow for the possibility of the lamp or candle staying lit throughout the service.

The movement of the Lamplighter should be unhurried and somewhat solemn, to create a sense of anticipation.

(**Reader** *is on stage with Bible open ready to read*)

(*Enter* **Lamplighter** *carrying the light. Places the light on the stand. Steps back one pace and looks at it approvingly. Steps forward and lifts cover from floor and places it over the lights. Exit.*)

Reader: (Luke 8:16-17) No one after lighting a lamp covers it with a vessel, or puts it under a bed, but puts it on a stand, that those who enter may see the light. For nothing is hid that shall not be made manifest, nor anything secret that shall not be known and come to the light.

(*Enter* **Lamplighter**. *Removes cover from the light and exits.*)

CHAPTER FOUR: Music

When children are present among the church that is praising God and they are enabled to participate, their relationship to God is nurtured and they will grow in their faith. Among the elements of the service, music is one that is not dependent on intellectual understanding. Children can participate in the musical offering of the church long before they can understand the sermon or follow the Eucharistic prayer. In the music of the service children are enabled to offer praise, in joy and adoration, in reverence and wonder. Similarly qualities of love, friendship, and caring are learned among the church members and children grow to associate those qualities with the Christian faith.

Music is a vital aspect of the worship life of the church, taking the affective in the human life and making opportunity to offer this in thanksgiving and praise to God. Often there are responses offered to God that would find no other means of communication. In one church I visited, one member who found it incredibly difficult to express his response to God in words, said, ''I can't really put my thoughts into words but I can put them into songs.'' He went on to say how important particular familiar songs were to him. He saw too the need for each worshipping church to have an established repertoire of songs that facilitated praise, and how carefully new music should be introduced to enhance and add to that repertoire in order that this function of carrying or embodying the praise of the people should not be lost to them.

Hence, those who lead the music in church worship should have an understanding of the function of music, the relevance of the music in any particular service. They should have a depth of communication with the church members that makes both the developing repertoire and particular selections very relevant to the overall worship life of the church. This requires open and creative communication between the music leader and other worship leaders, and with church members of all ages.

Everyone should be enabled to offer and respond to God. Music is chosen and led so that all have an opportunity to participate and will be selected to help the congregation worship. The established repertoire of music includes songs and hymns that express the various moods of the congregation as well as the themes of the lectionary and the seasons of the Church year. New music will be included with consideration for the congregation and what facilitates their worship.

Church music is not there only to please the musicians, choirs and music groups. Their approach must be primarily to serve the people and facilitate their relationship to God. This can be a frustration to musicians who may wish to be more musically adventurous than the congregation can be. Music leadership is both a calling and an anointing in any congregation; the musicians must have reached the point of offering their gift to serve the people, and the best music leaders for worship may not always be the most proficient musicians in the congregation.

The Repertoire

In establishing a repertoire for all age worship, look for breadth of musical style and form, of contemporary and traditional, representing the heritage and the variety of Christian experience.

The primary work of God's people is to praise. With the saints and angels, God's people join in singing "Amen! Blessing and glory and wisdom and thanksgiving and honor and power and might be to our God for ever and ever! Amen." (Revelation 7:11,12). Look among the best of ancient and modern hymns of majestic praise and glory to join in singing this praise. Look out for music that reflects that praise is not offered with ulterior motive, is not essentially a request but is praise of the creator as the source of life, in a cycle of love that comes from God and is offered reciprocally by his people. A beautiful traditional hymn that carries this theme is "When morning guilds the skies, /My heart awaking cries, /May Jesus Christ be praised," (AM 223). The Eucharistic service commonly includes the Gloria which is a great hymn to the Trinity, that may be spoken or sung by the congregation.

God calls and the people respond with obedience and faithfulness. This will be expressed through music as well as in prayers and movement. As God speaks, the people declare their commitment to his word and his call. Many times this response is gathered into a song as well as in the words of the Creed.

There is a traditional hymn which uses words now less familiar, "New every morning is the love /Our wakening and uprising prove; /Through sleep and darkness safely brought, /Restored to life and power and thought." (AM 4). The hymn goes on to express more fully a quality of reverence for ordinary daily life and ends in a prayer that asks God for grace to live more faithfully in a more integrated daily life.

Thankfulness is offered to God, for the whole spectrum of human experience, from the ordinary toil of everyday work to the high points that are occasional. Thanksgiving may be expressed in choruses like "Thank you Lord..." (SLW 113), or in hymns like "Now thank we all our God" (AM 374).

Intercession for others and our willingness to serve Christ in the people we encounter may be sung in "Lord give us your Spirit," (CH 52), or "Neighbours" (CH 88).

Other prayers may be presented in music. Consider the prayer of St Francis and the Lord's Prayer which have been set to music. In *Cry Hosanna* songbook is a setting of the Lord's Prayer that is excellent for all age worship. At first viewing the music may seem just too difficult. But don't be deterred. The music is complex, but once learned with the accompanying actions, all ages from babes in arms are drawn into praise and worship.

Throughout their history God's people have offered praise with music. From the writing of the psalms and their place in Old Testament worship we see the extent of that history. To choose material for worship that reflects that heritage helps the members of the church identify themselves with the Church past and present and have some concept of themselves in the movement of God on the earth since the beginning of time. This enriches the life of the church. Even a tiny or struggling congregation is encouraged when enabled to recognise its unique place in a gathering of people whose history and experience stretches back over thousands of years, and will stretch as far into the future. There are many great and timeless hymns that come from that heritage. The psalms are the oldest and may be sung in modern settings, or spoken by the congregation. The chanting of psalms is now very uncommon; however, if you wish to use chanted music do so gradually, like any other new music, and only continue if this really does help the worship. The chants from the Community at Taizé are now being used by many congregations.

People of many languages and cultures are worshipping God. Even more than adults, children enjoy singing hymns in other languages, and this for all the congregation recalls the activity of the Spirit in the Church and the world today. Again it is a great encouragement to a congregation when enabled to grasp an impression of themselves as members of the vast body of God's people around the world.

Elements of contemporary popular music can be effective in worship. They have the advantage of being a familiar form for people. For congregational worship, such music should remain straightforward and meaningful. Do not lose the focus of worship by being too trendy. The music must serve as a vehicle for worship. The rock and folk idioms should be considered and worship resources carefully selected. Much of the music written in these idioms is written for presentation by a soloist or small group and may or may not enhance corporate worship; use them selectively.

Avoid songs that are simplistic in their music or their words. Find music that is simple but at the same time is musically acceptable to both musicians and congregation. As God's people we want to offer our best to him. In our church music, we have an opportunity to introduce music that helps all ages grow in their experience and appreciation of music. Find music that represents a broad spectrum, from the occasional song that is almost simple as a nursery rhyme, to music that is more challenging to church people who have had some musical education and experience. In a mixture of these, and everything in-between, a congregation may be led corporately, not as a series of interest or age groups, but together.

Look at the words of the songs and hymns. Some may be simple and childlike, but avoid the mistake of introducing children to words that are simplistic and patronising. Some collections of children's hymns are full of words like "little" and "nice". They do not on the whole enhance the worship of a congregation of all ages. There are occasions to sing "Two little eyes to look to God," but not very often. Do not be afraid of hymns and songs that use vocabulary beyond the present speaking vocabulary of children in the congregation. All of us extend our vocabulary by meeting words in their everyday usage, knowing their meaning from the context in which they happen. Children will learn the meaning of such words as "reverence" and "majesty" by the context and way in which the church uses them. Look at a selection of children's stories at the local library for an impression of the extensive vocabulary that can be used with children. If the music leadership really has the interests of the people at heart and does serve them in music, it is possible to say that they should avoid words or music that are too simplistic for them to be able to worship with themselves.

Selecting Music

In planning, the music should fit with the theme of the service (seasonal and specific), should express the needs and concerns of the congregation, and fit the form of the service, whether informal or formal, whether Morning Prayer or Eucharist.

The guidelines in Chapter Three and in Chapter Thirteen are relevant here also.

Different pieces of music fit into different parts of the service, either stylistically or in the overall qualities of the song, fitting the mood of the congregation and the movement of the service. The words are not the only factor in selection, though they are important: the music itself must fit appropriately. Sometimes churches find themselves using a simple song such as "Seek ye first the Kingdom of God" in times of quiet praise and worship when the intended focus is on God not the congregation. The music seems fitting to such times. However, the words are addressed to the congregation, and have primarily a teaching message.

At the beginning of a service choose a song or hymn that people know well and can sing wholeheartedly. The music can help establish a friendly atmosphere of belonging and can enhance the Call to Worship.

Some churches effectively include a short selection of easy and relaxing songs to draw people together. Ensure that such times make sense liturgically. It is not necessary, if the music and worship leaders are fully concerned with all age worship to insert a slot of "children's" songs, suggesting that it is necessary to address them separately from the rest of the congregation. To do so could break down the understanding of being people of God together, and cause an unhelpful and unnecessary break in the liturgy or flow of the service. If you are planning to use a brief selection of chorus-type songs consider how they fit liturgically with the service, what effect they have for the congregation (ask them for their opinion—adults and children—don't make assumptions) and which songs will be most effective in expressing praise at this point in the service. In some worship settings, a medley of choruses has the effect of re-establishing an atmosphere or friendship and fellowship.

Around the Bible reading and sermon, one expects to find songs that are topical, seasonal or are psalms. These should lead towards what is to be said, in feeling as well as in content of the words. "Joy in the Lord" (SLW 97) and "Bless thou the Lord" (SLW 104) are examples of contemporary psalm settings. Look for songs such as "On Jordan's Bank" (SLW 117), "Wake Up" (SLW 116) and "The Wedding Banquet" (SLW 115), which have a seasonal theme which will relate to the readings. Some Bible stories have been turned into songs, and this point of the service is an ideal time to use them.

In every service there is an offertory, usually with a hymn. This position in the liturgy is the time for the people's response to God, offering themselves - not only their money.

More often a fairly strong hymn is most suited, though occasionally the sermon requires reflection and quieter song may be suitable. Consider "Canticle of the Gift" (SLW2), "God has spoken" (SLW 95), "Alleluia, Give thanks to the risen Lord" (SLW 1), as well as traditional hymns such as "Alleluia, sing to Jesus" (AM 399).

During the administration of Communion quiet songs of praise and worship are appropriate, both traditional and modern eucharistic music: "Hallelujah my Father" (FS 6) and "Glory be to Jesus" (SLW 68).

The end of the service is marked by a hymn, during which the choir and ministers process out. Their movement is symbolic of the liturgy at this point: the movement of the people of God out into the world. The hymn reflects that theme, the people expressing their calling to be the body of Christ in their everyday life.

Abbreviations:

AM— *Hymns Ancient and Modern Revised*
SLW— *Sound of Living Waters*
FS— *Fresh Sounds*
CH— *Cry Hosanna*

CHAPTER FIVE: The Word of God: Readings

When John wrote down his gospel account, he spoke of the Word of God and used the Greek word *Logos*, which meant both the spoken word and the thought and reason which was expressed in words. Greek philosophers, believing that the universe is essentially rational, used *Logos* to communicate this rational principle. When John wrote that the "word became flesh," he was saying that the essential order of the universe became present in human form within the universe. As a result, Jesus saw the order and truth of life and spoke about what he saw, about what he lived and about his own identity. He did this so others might begin to see and understand the order of life and fulfil their own part in that order.

The word of God in the Church is a continuing unveiling of the unity of creation. The body of Christ looks to the future for the time when it will reach "the fulness of him who fills all in all" (Ephesians 1:23). In the meantime, the Church is imperfect and incomplete, but the word of God carries the Church forward toward that time, always becoming more fully the body of Christ.

The prophetic word of God in church tells of what is at present and what is to come. It points to the continuing work and order of God. The prophetic word speaks of what God is doing. Truly to hear the word is to receive the grace to work out that word. The body of Christ is the expression of the word in the flesh, though incomplete. While the prophetic word does look forward to the "fullness of time," it is a topical and contemporary word which takes the body of believers on, in growing towards maturity.

The word that teaches reveals and describes the essential order of God in the universe. This is the law and this word stands through history. As this word is heard, the people of God will understand themselves more fully, how they are becoming a visible presence in the world—that the world may see and believe for themselves. The prophetic word will always fit with this; a true prophecy will always be in harmony with the order of God's purpose for his creation.

When the word of God is spoken, what we hear is a recollection or description in our language and concepts of what God is actually creating and doing. It is as if the speaker or reader is an eye-witness to the word.

Such understanding, therefore, affects the presentation of Bible readings and teachings and sermons during the all-age worship service. Firstly, the presentation of the word is far too serious a matter for it to be treated lightly, just because the church has younger members present. The sermon may at times be serious and profound but it is vitally important that it is both coherent and intelligible. Since our experience of the word of God is in the incarnation of Christ, in the creation and the ongoing embodiment of the word in the Church, it is immensely appropriate that the presentation of the word is not only spoken but visible. It is important to the people that they are participants in speaking the word and see themselves embodying that word.

God's Word is for the people, to mould them and make them into God's people. The word is for adults and children, old, young, and handicapped. The presentation of the word should take into account ways that enable everyone to hear, for to hear the word is to receive the grace to do it. Hearing the word is not an intellectual process though it includes the intellect; having an intellectual appreciation of the word of God is not the same living by the word.

Presentation

When the Bible is read, the reader should be one who is able to present the words clearly and simply. The reader does not over-emphasise, interpret or preach. The reading will speak for itself. For people who are reading in church for the first time give the opportunity to rehearse.

The presentation of the Word in Scriptures can be developed in other ways that refresh the meaning for the hearer. Adopt these ways in addition to straightforward reading on appropriate occasions.

Retelling for ourselves the story of our history as God's people, according to the lectionary, and according to seasons of the church, continues to tell us who we are as God's people, helps us understand what it means to be people of God. There are many ways to bring alive our story. We can hear it, and stories are more memorable than other spoken words. But remember, Bible stories may be glossed over as they are very familiar. It is easy for the listeners to switch off and find themselves daydreaming. Stories may be re-enacted for us, in which case we will probably remember them well. Puppets, dramas, mimes and dramatic readings may be presented for the congregation.

It is also possible for the congregation to re-enact the story themselves, building a drama in which all take part. As they are all part of making the story, they remember it and its meaning will become part of them. A much quoted proverb says, "We hear and we forget, we see and we remember, we do and we understand."

So it is possible for the presentation of the word of God to use, in addition to the Bible readings, rehearsed plays retelling bible stories and parables, congregational drama and reading, puppet plays, rehearsed or spontaneous.

The scripts in this chapter are all ways of retelling Bible stories, through readings. The following chapters: "Bible Stories: Drama" and "Bible Stories: with Puppets" similarly include the retelling of Bible stories, with notes on preparing them for use in church. Chapter 8 includes scripts that interpret the Scriptures using contemporary situations.

Each script includes notes on preparation and presentation. Rehearse the readings well, noting if the congregation will also need preparation during the service.

OLD DRY BONES

A reading for the congregation, based on Ezekial 37:1-14. The chorus is rehearsed together and a reader leads the verses.

Characters: Reader

Rehearse as follows: The Reader says the chorus once and asks the congregation to join with her in repeating it.

The Reader tells the congregation that every time it happens in the story the chorus is said through twice, "so let's try that now." They say it together twice.

The Reader then asks the congregation to add finger snaps, light clapping or foot tapping rhythms as they say the chorus twice more.

The reader now asks the congregation to keep the clapping rhythm going not only for the chorus but during the verse as well.

Reader: (*Chorus*)

Old dry bones, old dry bones,
Hear the word of the Lord.

(*repeat*)

1. Down in the valley
   It was full of old bones,
   They were stacked up there
   Just piles of dead bones.

Congregation:

(*Chorus*)

Reader:

2. Now God, He said,
   "I'll make them live,
   I'll join them together
   And I'll fill them with breath."

Congregation:

(*Chorus*)

Reader:

3. So I prophesied
   As I was told
   And those old dry bones
   Stood side by side.
   They stood right up
   And the meat appeared,
   They were covered in skin,
   But they were still dead.

Congregation:

(*Chorus*)

Reader:

4. So I prophesied
   Till the wind then blew,
   And those people came alive
   Just like they were new.

Congregation:

(*Chorus*)

WHOM SHALL I SEND

A group reading based on Isaiah 6:1-8

Characters: Readers 1, 2, 3, 4

The reading is strong and proclamatory throughout. The Readers should rehearse the script several times together, and ensure that there is a smooth, though not rapid, flow from line to line.

1:	In the year that King Uzziah died
1,2:	I saw the Lord
4:	(*majestically*) Sitting upon a throne
1,2,3:	High and lifted up
All:	And his train filled the temple.
3:	Above him stood the seraphim; Each had six wings
4:	(*lightly*) With two he covered his face
2:	(*lightly*) With two he covered his feet

1: And with two he flew.

3: And one
4: Called to another
2: And said
All: (*with awe*) "Holy, holy, holy
Is the Lord of Hosts,
And the whole earth
Is full of his glory."

4: And the foundations of the thresholds
2,3,4: Shook
4: At the voice of him who called
1: And the house was filled with smoke.

3: And I said
1: "Woe is me, for I am lost,
4: For I am a man of unclean lips
1,3: And I dwell in the midst of a people
1,3,4: Of unclean lips.
1: For my eyes have seen the King,
All: The Lord of Hosts."

1: Then flew one of the seraphim to me,
4: Having in his hand a burning coal,
3: Which he had taken with tongs
2: From the altar.
1: And he touched my mouth
And said,
All: "Behold,
2: This has touched your lips,

4: Your guilt is taken away,
2: And your sin forgiven."

3: And I heard the voice of the Lord saying,
1: "Whom shall I send,
And who will go for us?"
2: Then I said,
4: "Here am I,
All: Send me."

KING HEZEKIAH

A congregational reading based on II Chronicles 29—31.

Characters: Hezekiah, Priests and Levites, People (the congregation), Narrator

A congregational script should be prepared beforehand. The necessary phrase could be included in the service sheet, or on an overhead projector.

Narrator: Many years had passed since the days of King David and his wise son Solomon who had reigned after him. There had been many unfaithful kings who had led the people away from God. Ahaz had been one more terrible king, but his son Hezekiah was different. Hezekiah wanted to serve the true God, just as David had done many years before.
With this in mind, Hezekiah gathered all the Priests and Levites into the square outside the temple. The building was now dishevelled and almost derelict, more like an old barn than a temple.

Hezekiah: You are the Priests of Jahweh, the one true God, and you should be serving him faithfully. Make yourselves holy before God, repair your ways so as to be fit for the work you do for him.
Clean out the temple! Remove the filth and rubbish! Make the temple a place of beauty for God.

Narrator: So the Priests and Levites cleaned the temple, carrying out all the dirt and rubbish, and washed it all away in a brook which flowed nearby.

Priests & Levites: We have cleaned the temple, the altars and the dishes. Look, all is ready for worship.

Narrator: So the King and the Priests and Levites dedicated the temple with sacrifice and worship. Those who gathered sang and praised the Lord.

Priests & Levites: Praise the Lord our God, for he is good. God has forgiven us, for he is good.

Narrator: They sang the psalms of David, singing with gladness and bowing down to worship God. Hezekiah and his government decided that to celebrate the Passover all the people of Israel should be summoned to Jerusalem.

Priests & Levites: (*addressing the congregation*) O people of Israel, return to worship the Lord. God will be gracious and merciful to you.

Narrator: Many of the people came to Jerusalem for the celebration of the Passover in the temple. So magnificent and so exciting was the celebration that the people stayed on for an extra seven days. All who gathered were blessed by the Priests and Levites, and God heard their worship and praise.

Narrator: Hezekiah led the people back to God, he did what was good. And everything he did for God he did with his whole heart.

Hezekiah: We must all bring gifts to God, our first fruits and tithes, to establish again the work of the temple. Bring your gifts to the house of the Lord.

People:
We are bringing our grain and our wine.
We are bringing our oil and our honey.
We are bringing our tithes and our offerings.
We bring our gifts to God.

RUTH AND NAOMI

A dramatic reading.

Characters: Ruth, Naomi, Narrator
This script is used like a radio play, with the players reading appropriately.

Narrator: (*Read Ruth 1:1-5*)

Naomi: My dear, I think I'll go back to Israel. I'm tired of this land with all its strange ways, and everything is far too busy. I'm going back where I belong.

Ruth: Don't you belong here where we all love you?

Naomi: Not really, I'll go home to my kinsfolk, and maybe I'll get back my interest in life.

It's a terrible thing for your husband and your sons to die in a foreign land. No, I'm going back where I am understood and I know the ways.

There are lots of places we used to walk when I was a child and I'd like to see them again. I'd like to see the people I grew up with.

I would like to pack and go fairly soon. It would be good to be home.

Ruth: What will we do when we get there? Where will we live? Tell me what is it like? Is it very different?

Naomi: Oh, you won't be coming. You'll stay here. This is your country.

Ruth: But I'd rather go with you than be here.

Naomi: You would not want to be a foreigner in Israel now, especially a Gentile. No, you stay here.

Ruth: Could I become a Jew and really get to be one of your people?

Naomi: You wouldn't, not you. Now if you didn't believe in your own gods, you might manage it more easily.

Ruth: I want to do it. I can't let you go back on your own.

Naomi: Don't be silly. No one can do it. You can't change your whole way of living. You could never be Jewish.

Ruth: I don't think that's true—I want to be with you, so I can get used to things being different.

Naomi: But don't you see; you can never change from being a Moabite. You will always like Moabite food and music. You will want to see the mountains and fields you grew up with. It is not possible to change that much.

Ruth: Look I'm not going to Israel just so I can be Jewish. It's to be in your family—you and me together.

Naomi: That's what I am saying too. You can't be Jewish and like our ways and our food and everything so much that it will feel like home. You can't help loving what you have grown up with. That's all there is to it!

Ruth: What I am saying is that I love you and I care about you. My friends think it's silly that I am such good friends with my mother-in-law. And maybe it is strange. But what I know is that, even though my husband is dead, you still feel like the only real family that I have. I am still much closer to you than I am to my own mother. So I want to go with you, wherever you go.

Naomi: (*slowly*) Do you realise you may never come back. Israel is not the safest place for foreigners. There is a lot of prejudice. You had better stay here, love.

Ruth: Well, you are going back and if it wouldn't be safe for me it wouldn't be safe for you. It's all the same.

Naomi: But it isn't the same. They are my people; I grew up

29

with them, played with them and danced with them. Now I shall grow old with them. They are my folks.

Ruth: If they are your people, then they are my people and if you can grow old there, so can I. I belong with you and where you go I will go.

Narrator: So Naomi returned to Israel and Ruth went with her. They set out together to Naomi's home town, Bethlehem. On their arrival they found a place to live but they were very poor as they had no way of earning a living.
They arrived in Bethlehem at the time of the barley harvest. The local people remembered Naomi and asked about her sadness. She told them of the death of her husband and of her two fine sons. They asked her who the strange woman was who accompanied her. Naomi told them this was her Moabite daughter-in-law.

Naomi: We have no money and must get some food for ourselves. It is too late to plant a crop, so we shall have to depend on the help of others.

Ruth: Let me go into the fields and glean behind the workers who harvest the barley. I will bring home some food.

Narrator: Ruth went into the fields and worked hard from dawn till dusk, picking up the heads of barley that fell from the sheaves. Then the owner of the land came out to the field to look at his harvest. He asked the workers in the field who this young woman was who gleaned the corn in his field. They told him this was Ruth the Moabitess. He instructed the workers to leave extra heads of corn lying on the ground for her, because he had heard of Ruth's dedication to Naomi. So Ruth was able to take home food for herself and Naomi.

WINTER PSALM

This simple reading was prepared for a Christmas morning service when lots of children were to be present.

Characters: Reader

The congregation joins in the second line to each verse. The reader should first explain their part to them. More verses may be added.

Reader:
With crunchy frost and crackling ice-
We will praise the Lord.

With grey-clad skies and falling snow-
We will praise the Lord.

In gloves and scarves and hats and coats-
We will praise the Lord.

With friendly cries and joyful hearts-
We will praise the Lord.

With carols, fellowship and fun-
We will praise the Lord.

CHAPTER SIX: Bible Stories: Drama

Learning by doing

People learn through what they do, that's not only children but adults too.

Drama, because of its inherent quality of 'doing', is an ideal experiential form for discovering, investigating, experimenting with, and reflecting on the meaning of life, on human values and qualities. These are essential concerns of moral, ethical and religious education and of the church which wishes to be formed by God into a people for his purposes.

Most under-sixes, and some older children, do not understand what is happening in performance. If they are watching, it is real. If they are involved, it is a live experience, unpredictable and open-ended. In the same way, young children can be unsure that a story in a book has a fixed ending. However, they do enjoy taking a small part in drama presentations with others who are older.

Older children often enjoy entertaining others, as they appreciate the nature of the illusory and dramatic. Participation should include a variety of possibilities, as some will not wish to be on stage. They may enjoy working as stewards, hosts, stage hands, and production assistants.

With teenagers, drama may be used as a tool for reflection on meaning, values and attitudes. The adult may set a problem that challenges and leads to discussion. Roles and problems are set, so that young people may investigate inner pressures and reactions, reconsider personal attitudes, and grow to understand other people.

Telling or retelling the story of the history of God's people, according to the lectionary and according to the seasons of the Church, helps the congregation know their identity. It is good for all members of the church to know and appreciate not just Bible stories but the stories of saints and the Church's history after Bible times, as their history and heritage. Ideally, since they learn through what they do, they will find many ways to participate in the stories at adult and child level. As they are all part of making the story they remember it and its relevance is more apparent.

Use rehearsed plays retelling Bible stories and parables; use congregational drama and reading; try puppet plays, rehearsed or spontaneous.

Mix ages together wherever possible when using drama in church. If a play is suitable only for children to take part, it may well not be appropriate for use with the church as a whole.

The mixing of ages together affirms the membership and partnership of all ages in the life of the church and the equal need of all to learn and be nurtured in faith.

Remember, however, that the worship service is the context for an encounter between God and his people. If drama is being used it should enhance that encounter, not direct attention away from God. Do not make children or drama the centre of attention but include the drama in the congregation's experience of God.

Avoid sentimentality; it kills the reality of God's relationship with each person present and ultimately devalues and patronises the people present.

A Christmas play, for example, has a valid place in the life of the Church, to recollect the reality of God taking humanity upon himself, to re-enact the story in a way that touches the people's hearts, to look again at the profound simplicity of the gospel story without the commercialisation associated with the contemporary celebration of the festival, to praise and worship God for his place in history and his gift of life and redemption. Therefore do not be sentimental, don't do the play because "It is sweet," or "The children like it, don't they?" If the play has little relevance to the life and faith of the church don't put it in the context of worship.

Drama

For a performance during worship, use a scripted play. Writing your own play can be an option if you have experience of working with drama and know the parameters within which to work. If you have no experience, use established material.

For those new to drama, choose very simple, or short and easy plays that do not depend on clever acting or presentation. The audience will be happy to imagine what is not there, if they know the story, so choose a presentation of a well-known story for the first attempt. Be more adventurous as the abilities of the group become more apparent.

When the play is for a Church festival, such as Christmas or Mothering Sunday, choose a script that includes the simple retelling of a Bible story or of something foundational in Christian experience. Many of those who come to watch will have never heard or have forgotten the original story, so a basic retelling is best for the audience. Interpretation is best in a postscript, or in an accompanying reading or sermon.

For whatever occasion, ensure that you are choosing material that is appropriate to all your actors. For example, don't use scripted words for non-readers, use a narrative form with mimed parts. Avoid choosing teens material with younger children in the group, as the humour can be too sophisticated and the reflective process beyond their scope. If in doubt ask children in the group if they like the material; if they don't like it, you're onto a loser.

Developing a script improvisation

Occasionally the group may develop the script ideas together, in an improvisation. This may be taped or noted, written up and edited until it can be used as a script for performance.

I used this method when some older Sunday School children were tired of the sameness of Christmas nativity plays. The younger children were still becoming familiar with the story which was retold each year in a nativity play. Set in the annual Christingle service, a nativity play of some kind was thematically most fitting. But the older children wanted a play with space travellers. So together they helped develop a simple nativity play in which younger children were the actors. Around this we built the secondary script of the space travellers watching the event with curiosity. The script of space travellers was the slightly edited and more structured version of the children's own suggested conversation. (The script is in Chapter Seventeen).

When using improvisation, the following starting point may be used:
Use a well known story that the group can play out freely, trying on the characters and the dilemmas in which they are involved.

Tell the whole story, to give the complete span.

List and choose characters, including the group members in the choice and letting them discuss differences of opinion.

Retell a small part of the story, and dramatise. Then take next scene.

Having developed each new scene redo the previous scenes with the new one on the end.

Preparation of play

If you have chosen a scripted play for use in all age worship you should cover the following points carefully:

Characters: How many are needed? Do the sexes fit your group? In a mixed group, you will probably find that girls will play male roles but boys will not so readily play female roles.

When wanting to include God in a story, it may be best to keep to a voice offstage, as it is very awkward to represent him in person. Don't be discouraging if the members of your group create a character for God or choose his 'voice' according to traditional stereotypes; don't be tempted to manipulate them into doing something which you as an adult would like to experiment with. However, one eleven-year-old boy carefully explained to me about plays featuring God, "God is neither a man or a woman, so it depends who you can get."

Costumes: What is your source for costumes? Look at jumble sales as a source of various garments for a basic wardrobe. Acquire some gold card with button jewels for a variety of crowns. You might ask a small group to provide costumes, giving them guidelines of how you would like them to be made. Look at local fancy dress shops or costumiers, but this is a more expensive option. You could gather a group of adults who are prepared to sew to your specifications, using materials from 'free' sources such as jumble sales.

Make props from card or paper as realistically as possible. Many items can be made of papier maché, but use real items if possible, e.g. telephone, clock, plates.

For scenery, backdrops may be helpful. Try painting the scene on paper or an old sheet, or acquire a roll of corrugated card which may be unrolled to the various scenes needed. (see References p. 136)

Allow plenty of time for rehearsal, for memorising parts, for developing sets and props.

Plan a schedule that makes sense for all group members. If scenes include only two or three characters, rehearse with them when the others are working at something else. If group members are required to watch for long periods without being active themselves, they will be bored and cause disturbance. Try bringing the Crowd in for later rehearsals.

Plan several rehearsals for familiarisation, then several for serious development of character and movements. Then develop further in costume, as the actors feel the part more fully when dressed for it: everyone thinks themselves more noble when wearing a crown.

Always include at least one full rehearsal on the final set. A change of environment can upset the most settled group. Entrances and exits may need to be reassigned and rehearsed in the new place. Voices may need to be raised. Give children a turn at listening at the back of the church so they realise how quietly the group members are speaking.

Directing and Producing

To encourage better performance, relate the characterisation to examples within the personal experience of those taking part. Point out aspects of the setting that the characters might relate to more in showing their reactions.

Drama is movement as well as spoken word; feelings are body actions as well as shouts or cries. Help characters use their bodies: you might rehearse the scene with only the movement and gestures of the group members, no spoken words.

Leadership

Keep open-ended in your conversations with the group members; the performance is never more important than your fellowship.

Let the group help develop the qualities of the characters, through experiment and reflection.

Allow mistakes to be made.

Never trick, violate, tease, create fear, or cause mistrust. Instead, inspire, motivate and encourage your cast.

Listen first and engage in real conversation. Do not indoctrinate.

Examine your attitude to all group members as persons in, their own right. Consider the attitude with which you approach them.

Practical notes

Consider using some form of special lighting; the effect is always to create an expectant atmosphere. Several goose-neck lamps or household spotlights can be sufficient for simple productions when well placed.

STORM AT SEA

A drama for the congregation, based on Mark 4:36-41.

Characters: Reader, Leaders for sections A,B,C,D

The congregation is divided into four groups, to follow Leaders of A,B,C,D. The Leaders should be well rehearsed beforehand. The Reader should rehearse each section of the congregation in following the appropriate leader before beginning the play.

Group A—makes a rainstorm. Tap one finger on the opposite hand. As Leader directs they follow, changing to two fingers, then three, then full hand when storm is greatest.

Group B—make whistling and whooshing noises (wind and waves), raising sound gradually as leader lifts hand. Practice stopping when Leader drops hand.

Group C—Two or three people use large sheets of card which when shaken make noises of thunder. Start with one person and gradually add others.

Group D—Follow Leader in all actions as in script.

Props: Large sheets of card

Reader:

The disciples rowed across the sea,
As the sun sank in the west.
And after a long and busy day,
(D *begins rowing*)
Jesus took a rest.

Before very long he was fast asleep,
There was hardly any sound.
Just the murmurs of the working men
And the lap of waves on the bow.
(B *begins whooshing*)

Dark clouds hid the shining moon,
(D *rocks with boat*)
Blotting out the stars.
The wind rose to a blustery squall
And drops of rain fell hard.
(*All sounds begin*)

The wind grew stronger, blowing a gale,
It drove the crashing waves;
(D *rocks wildly*)
The rain came down in torrents
The air was filled with noise.
(C *increase sound*)

All the men were scared to death,
Around them raged the storm;

(C *full sound*)
The thunder roared, the lightning flashed,
(D *falling around*)
They feared that they would drown.

"Save us, Lord," the disciples cried,
(*Hands upward*)
"We're dying one and all!"
Jesus woke, saw the fearsome storm
"Peace, be still," he called.
(*All sounds stop on 'Still', as Narrator raises hand high*)

The great storm died, the waves fell back,
The tossing boat was safe.
He asked them then "Where is your faith?"
But they were so amazed,
"Just how important is this man
Who rules the wind and waves?"

CROSSING THE RED SEA

A congregational drama, based on Exodus 14.

Characters: Reader, Israelites, Egyptians.

Props: each member or pair of the congregation should be provided with a copy of the congregational script on page 37.

Divide the congregation down the middle into two groups, designating one group to be Israelites and one the Egyptians.

(Or let them choose). Rehearse each side in one verse of the script; the last line is repeated, with the congregation coming in after the phrase "Oh dear," "Oh no," or "Oh Yes"; the lines in *italic* are spoken by the Israelites, those in CAPITALS by the Egyptians. If people are hesitant, encourage them to put feeling into their words as the story unfolds.

Avoid telling the congregation the ending of this story in advance; there are often some younger members for whom it is a surprise.

Reader:
    Long, long ago in ancient days
    Moses was Israel's head man.
    God told him to lead them from Egypt's land
    So he led them by God's plan.

Congregation:
    Oh yes, *he led us by God's plan.*

    Out in the desert toward the east
    They walked in one great line,
    To escape the Egyptians who wanted slaves;
    But would they escape in time?

Congregation:
    Oh dear, *can we escape in time?*

    They rounded a hill of sand and rock
    And before them they saw the sea.
    It was red and huge, from north to south,

And the Egyptians were right behind.

Congregation:
    Oh yes, WE EGYPTIANS ARE RIGHT BEHIND.

    Well, here they come those Egyptian men
    With chariots, swords and whips.
    They wanted these slaves to do their work,
    To build their great pyramids.

Congregation:
    Oh yes, TO BUILD OUR GREAT PYRAMIDS.

    The Israelite folk were very scared
    But Moses he wanted calm.
    He thought that now they ought to pray,
    Could God keep them safe from harm?

Congregation:
    Oh dear, *can God keep us safe from harm?*

    The thunderous marching drew very near,
    With shouting and yelling so grim.
    They'd round them up and whip them to shape,
    Get them back to making the bricks.

Congregation:
    Oh yes, GET THEM BACK TO MAKING THE BRICKS.

    The sea was wet and extremely cold
    As the first ones reached the edge.
    They'd drown. But goodness, it opened up;
    The water rolled back from the beach.

Congregation:
Oh yes, *the water rolled back from the beach.*

Forward they went with determined steps,
Moses he had said, "Pray."
Past walls of water they walked in the dry,
For God had said, "You go this way."

Congregation:
Oh yes, *God had said, "You go this way."*

The Egyptians now were quite upset,
Seething and angry and crazy.
They must not escape, these Israelite slaves;
They'd capture them all anyway.

Congregation:
Oh yes, WE'LL CAPTURE THEM ALL ANYWAY.

Into the sea path the soldiers rode,
The Israelites hurried along.
And thundering on came the soldiers behind.
To show them they'd gone wrong.

Congregation:
Oh yes, TO SHOW THEM THEY'VE GONE WRONG!

The Egyptians hurried, closing the gap,
But the Israelites reached the dry ground.
Just as they did, God let loose the waves,
Those Egyptians, they were all drowned!

Congregation:
Oh no, WE EGYPTIANS, WE ARE ALL DROWNED.

They stood on dry land, the Israelite folk,
They danced and shouted and cheered.
They all praised God, he had brought them safe
From the danger they had all feared.

Congregation:
Oh yes, *from the danger we had all feared.*

God called them out, he led them well
Through the peril of the great Red Sea.
They were anxious and puzzled, it all seemed wrong,
Yet God led them faithfully through.

Congregation:
Oh yes, *God led us faithfully through.*

CROSSING THE RED SEA

Congregational script.

Israelites' words are in *italic* script.
Egyptians' words are in CAPITALS.

Oh yes,
He led us by God's plan.

Oh dear,
Can we escape in time?

37

Oh yes,
WE EGYPTIANS ARE RIGHT BEHIND.

Oh yes,
TO BUILD OUR GREAT PYRAMIDS.

Oh dear,
Can God keep us safe from harm?

Oh yes,
GET THEM BACK TO MAKING THE BRICKS.

Oh yes,
The water rolled back from the beach.

Oh yes,
God had said 'You go this way.'

Oh yes,
WE'LL CAPTURE THEM ALL ANYWAY.

Oh yes,
TO SHOW THEM THEY'VE GONE WRONG!

Oh no,
WE EGYPTIANS, WE ARE ALL DROWNED.

Oh yes,
From the danger we had all feared.

Oh yes,
God led us faithfully through.

Permission is given for this page to be reproduced for congregational use during the presentation of this drama.

THROUGH THE DESERT

A congregational drama. It is based on Numbers 11:4—end, 14:26-35. The congregation imitate the actions of the Action Leader.

Characters: Reader, Action Leader.

The congregation should follow the actions of the Action Leader throughout the story, the Action Leader should therefore practise making large, clear and simple actions.

Reader:
  Twas early morning in the desert,
Action Leader:
  (*Yawn & stretch*)
  The ground was wet with dew,
  The drifting mist began to melt,
(*Rub eyes*)
  The sun was breaking through.

  The Israelites took down their tents,
(*Pull up pegs*)
  Their movements quick and steady;
  They called the kids, gathered their packs,
(*Beckon*)
  Soon all of them were ready.

  An early start so they could miss
(*Walk*)

The heat of the noonday sun.
Out on the trail from Egypt's land,
(*Nod to others*)
The long trek was begun.

The rising sun gave gentle heat
The skipping children sang;
(*Skip*)
An hour or two, then morning break
And calls for 'Orange' rang.
(*Wave and drink*)

"Water only," said the mums
(*Shake heads, 'no'*)
As men called out for tea.
"Biscuits too, with chocolate cream,"
(*Hand out*)
"Bread's all we've got," said they.

A mumbling grumble soon was heard,
Not just for orange and tea,
(*Mumbling*)
But meat and onion, Yorkshire pud,
And strawberries and cream.

"No more of them," old Moses said,
(*Hands 'no'*)
"We've left that all behind.
A simple lifestyle as we go,
(*Walk to side*)
No fancy meals with wine."

"Well if we'd known," the people said,
(*Cross arms indignantly*)
"We'd maybe never have come."
"I'd sooner be a well-fed slave,
(*Shaking arm angrily*)
Than poor and free," said one.

Now Moses had this vision
(*Wipes brow*)
Of a land so fair and free;
But how to take this grumbling bunch
(*Looks out*)
Was more than he could see.
(*Hand on side of head*)

So Moses prayed and talked to God,
(*Looks up*)
"The problem's this you know,
(*Hands up*)
They want to go to the Promised Land,
But pay the price, oh no!"
(*Shake head*)

"I'll send them meat," God said to him,
(*Hand out*)
"I'll send them chicken and wafers.
And no more complaints or I'll send them back,
To those nasty Egyptian slavers."
(*Peer to distance*)

Every day they collected bread
(*Collect wafers*)
And sometimes chicken for dinner.
But they forgot God, made a golden calf,
(*Rub tummy*)
As plainer food made them thinner.

Their grumbling rose to angry shouts
(*Fists up*)
And even God got cross.
But Moses pleaded "Don't give up,
(*Prays with hands up*)
Without you we are lost.
And people would say, 'Well that's no god,
(*Shrug*)
He couldn't get them across.' "

"Alright," said God, "I take your point,
(*Firm nod*)
But I will not change my plans.
None of these adults will ever see
(*Firm shake*)
My special Promised Land.

Only the children, who've learned from you
(*Beckon*)
And follow faithfully on,
Will I bring in to the Promised Land
(*Walk*)
On this journey so very long."

THE WALLS CAME TUMBLING DOWN

Narrative for use as a puppet play or with mime/drama, based on Joshua 6.

Since the play includes simple group action, very young children find it easy to join the drama, while adults and older children take the leading parts.

Characters: Reader, Joshua, two Spies, Israelites, People of Jericho

Props: Walls of Jericho: these may be constructed from heavy cardboard about 1 metre high, painted as a wall, and of sufficient size for several people to stand inside the walls.

If using this narrative with a puppet play, the walls are made from pieces of coloured card approximately 16x32 cms. The card is held by a stick in the left hand of the puppeteer, whose puppet looks over the top of this piece of wall. The puppeteers who are the People of Jericho hold the wall pieces close together each with a puppet looking over the top, giving the impression of a continuous city wall. Both puppets and walls may then fall at the appropriate moment.

Costumes: Simple biblical clothing.

Stage: Jericho should be located at the Centre Front of the church, with the People of Jericho standing within the walls when the play begins. The Israelites may begin at the back of the church, behind the congregation, coming up the aisle when crossing the river.

Very little rehearsal is necessary for this play. The Spies should creep surreptitiously. Joshua parts the river by holding his arms out in front of him then spreading them wide. The river should be at an agreed place half way up the aisle.

The congregation should join in the shout which is indicated by * in the script. Rehearse them immediately before the play, asking them to raise one hand and shout 'Hey!' very loudly after the Reader says "They shouted."

Reader:

One day God spoke; he'd been with these folk,
This itinerant wandering band,
"It's time," he said, "this is the time
To enter the Promised Land."

"Send some men to spy in Canaan,
Two fine men, you can choose.
(*Joshua sends the two Spies to look around Jericho*)
Tell them, 'See the kind of defences
People of Canaan use.' "

Those two men wandered round the city
Till people saw they were strangers.
(*People of Jericho point at Spies who hastily creep away*)
Then Rahab helped them escape that night
Safe from all the danger.

The two spies told the Israelites
About that Promised Land,
(*With lots of hand action Spies indicate the direction and size of Jericho*)

Then Joshua led them on their way
Down to Jordan's bank.

(*Israelites walk forward*)
The work was new to Joshua
But the river was parted soon,
(*Israelites stop as Joshua parts the river*)
From desert rough to Canaan shore
The Israelites marched through.

(*Israelites walk further*)
On they went with Joshua,
Not to the battle they'd have planned,
God said, "Walk around the town,
Round and round and round."

(*Begin to walk around the city*)
Round they went and still some more,
The townsfolk laughed and jeered.
(*The People of Jericho laugh and jeer noisily*)
Safe in their walls from enemy hordes,
Like a football crowd, they cheered.

"Alright," said Joshua, "on this day
(*Joshua and Israelites continue walking*)
We'll march round seven more
And when I raise my right hand high,
We'll shout like never before."

(*Joshua and Israelites stop walking. After "They shouted," Joshua raises his right hand and everyone shouts 'Hey'.*)

They shouted! * And the walls fell flat
(*People of Jericho push walls down from inside then fall themselves*)
And all the townsfolk with them.
This was the way to the Promised Land
A town for redevelopment.

WISE AND FOOLISH MAIDENS

A group drama, based on Matthew 25:1-13
This narration with mimed action and chorus needs little rehearsal.

Characters: Reader, Bridegroom, ten Maidens

Props: Ten lamps made of card: black on one side, gold, silver or white on the other; ten cards: on five is written 'Oil' on five is written 'No oil'.

Costumes: Contemporary, the Bridegroom may have a flower in his buttonhole.

Each Maiden is given a lamp. Five of them are given cards saying 'Oil.' The other five are given cards saying 'No oil.'

The Maidens hold up the lamps showing the lighted side at the beginning of the story. When the story says the maidens slept, they turn the dark side of the lamp outwards and close eyes to sleep. When the bridegroom knocks at the door they look at their cards to see if they have any oil. If they have, they relight the lamp. If they have no oil, they exit to buy some.

The congregation says the chorus with the reader during the presentation. As shown, the congregation is divided into two groups: rehearse their parts with them.

The congregation joins in the chorus of the reading. Half, designated A, repeat line two of the chorus and the others, designated B, repeat line three. Rehearse the congregation till this flows smoothly.

The Reader should keep a careful eye on the action to allow adequate time for actions such as reading cards.

(*Chorus*) **Reader**:
    There were
Group A:
    Five wise maidens and
Group B:
    Five foolish maidens there.

Reader:
    In olden days in Israel
    It was customary for
    Some maidens to greet the bridegroom
    And lead him through the door.

(*Chorus*)

    On this day there were maidens;
    Count them, there are ten.
    Each has a lamp and is ready
(*Hold up lamps*)

To show the bridegroom in.

(*Chorus*)

The bridegroom was late, the maidens slept,
(*Maidens sleep*)
The lamps used up the oil;
(*Turn lamps*)
Then at last when midnight came
The bridegroom knocked at the door.

(*Chorus*)

The maidens woke, their lamps were dead,
They all needed oil,
(*Read cards*)
But only some had brought a jar
Not enough to fill them all.

(*Chorus*)

The foolish maidens rushed away
(*Five Maidens hurry off*)
To try to buy some oil;
While they were gone the bridegroom came,
(*Bridegroom enters and crosses the stage, five Maidens lead him off*)
Five maidens led him in.

(*Chorus*)

Hurrying back, the foolish ones
(*Five Maidens return*)

At last had their lamps lit;
But they hadn't been ready all along
(*Sadly exit*)
And now it was too late.

(*Chorus*)

HORSES AND CHARIOTS OF FIRE

A narrative with congregational actions, based on II Kings 6:8-17.

Characters: Reader, Action Leader

Reader and Action Leader face the congregation. The congregation imitate all the movements of the Action Leader, so make the movements clear, big and simple.

Rehearse congregation in shouting "Help!" at appropriate moment in script and in cheering at the end.

Reader:
Long ago the Syrian king
Took his army out to war,
(*March*)
With shining swords and helmets strong
(*Pull sword from belt*)
Their victory was sure.

"Now this," he said, "will be the plan,
We'll attack that place today."
(*Point to distance*)

43

He wanted to conquer Israel
(*Cross arms confidently*)
Would everything go his way?
(*Nod firmly*)

Alas for him, Elisha, who
Was prophet in the land,
(*Hold up warning finger*)
Was listening hard for the word from God
(*Hand at ear*)
Who warned him of the plan.

Elisha sent a messenger
(*Beckon*)
To the king of Israel,
(*Point away*)
"Whatever you do, avoid this place
For Syria's marching through."
(*March*)

So every time he tried to attack
(*Throw spear*)
The Syrian king was foiled.
"How could this be? They know my plan.
(*Finger to brow*)
There must be a spy at court."
(*Finger outward*)

The king called his servants and asked them
"Which of you is a spy?"
(*Point along line*)

"My lord," they said, "it isn't us,
(*Shake head*)
Elisha's on their side!

They say their God knows everything
(*Tap head*)
Of what you think or say.
God tells it all to Elisha
Who prays to him day by day."
(*Hands in prayer*)

"Alright," cried the king, "then tell me,
Where is this terrible man?
(*Shake fist*)
We'll take our soldiers and chariots
We'll soon take care of him!"
(*Cut throat*)

Late that night they all went out
(*Tiptoe*)
Chariots, horses and men.
Surrounded the town where Elisha lived
(*Join hands*)
He didn't stand a chance.

Early in the morning,
(*Yawn and stretch*)
Elisha's servant looked out.
(*Hand shading eyes*)
He saw the terrible army
And gave an awful shout.

(*Shout "Help!"*)

"Elisha! Master, we've had it.
They'll get us, do us in."
(*Wring hands*)
But Elisha said, "Now don't be afraid
There's more of us than them."
(*Puzzled*)

So Elisha prayed and said to God
(*Hands up, pray*)
"Please show him what's really true."
God opened his eyes and showed him
(*Hands shading eyes*)
A truly marvellous view.
(*Hands out*)

Around them on the mountain
(*Hand out, circle*)
Was a vast and mighty crowd
Horses bold and chariots of fire
This was the army of God.
(*Hands up, cheer*)

BY THE SEA

A group play based on Mark 6:30-44.

Characters: Joseph, Sarah, Benjamin, Martha, Scribe, Pharisee, Narrator, Jesus, James, Philip, Matthew

Props: Basket containing bread rolls

Costumes: Biblical

(**Joseph** *and* **Benjamin** *enter.*)

Joseph:
Let's go and follow Jesus.

Benjamin:
Should we?

Joseph:
Yes, come on. Tell your mum first. You can have some of my lunch when you are hungry.

Benjamin:
Alright, I'll come.

(**Benjamin** *and* **Joseph** *freeze looking offstage to right.*)
(*Enter* **Sarah** *and* **Martha**.)

Sarah:
There they go. Let's follow Jesus.

Martha:
I think they are going into the country.

Sarah:
Do you think he is leaving us?

Martha:
No. But let's follow and see where he is going.

(**Sarah** *and* **Martha** *freeze looking offstage to right.*)

(*Enter* **Scribe** *and* **Pharisee**)

Scribe:

(*looking into distance*) He is going off in a boat now, and the people are following on the lakeside road.

Pharisee:

Herod will be pleased if we let him know what is happening. He thinks Jesus is a trouble maker.

(**Pharisee** *and* **Scribe** *freeze looking offstage to right.*)

Narrator:

Several thousand people followed Jesus and his disciples into the countryside near the Sea of Galilee. They did not know what to expect but they were curious and excited. They followed till they were dusty and tired. Then they sat on the rocky ground and listened to Jesus, who saw that they were like sheep without any shepherd.

(*Enter* **Jesus, James, Matthew, Philip**, *all Other Characters move to listen.*)

Matthew:

These people have been with us all day. They must be tired.

Jesus:

I expect they are hungry too. I don't expect they came prepared to be out all day.

James:

They should go into the local villages to buy food. But you will have to send them.

Jesus:

You give them something to eat.

Philip:

Thirty pounds would hardly buy enough bread, and we don't have that much money.

Jesus:

How many loaves have you got. Go and see.

(*As Disciples begin to search around* **Joseph** *and* **Benjamin** *go to the front of the crowd, furthest from* **Jesus**.)

Benjamin:

I'm hungry. Let's eat your food now.

Joseph:

That's a great idea. I'm starving.

Hang on though, I bet Jesus hasn't got any lunch. We could share our food with him.

(**Benjamin** *and* **Joseph** *cross stage to Disciples and* **Jesus**.)

Joseph:

Sir, would you like to share my lunch.

Andrew:

(*peering into the lunch bag*) He has some bread and some fish.

46

Benjamin:

It's not enough for everyone! It's for Jesus.

Jesus:

Do you mind if I share it with everyone? I think there will be enough.

Let's get everyone sitting on the grass.

(*holding up a bread roll*) Heavenly Father, thank you for the food you have given us. We ask you to bless the sharing of the bread among us. Amen.

(*Disciples hand out chunks of broken bread to all characters and then to the congregation.*)

TREASURES

A reading with mime, based on Matthew 6:19-22, 5:14,16.

Characters: Narrator, Woman, Man, Thief, Friend

Costumes: Thief can be costumed as a cat burglar, in black clothes, or with dark hat and scarf like a secret agent. Thief moves silently, with darting action, while frequently looking around to make sure no-one is chasing behind.

Props: Two small boxes clearly marked **Treasure**, that the congregation can easily read.

Notes: Action and words are simultaneous. Narrator should read clearly and firmly, finding a pace that allows those miming to keep their actions close to the reading. If, at the end of a verse, the actors have still to finish the relevant action, the Narrator should pause for them.

Narrator:

Do not lay up for yourselves treasures on earth, where moth and rust consume it and where thieves break in and steal it.

(**Woman** *enters carrying treasure box, is about to put it down when* **Thief** *creeps in to try to steal it.* **Woman** *dodges this way and that to avoid* **Thief** *getting the treasure.*)

But lay up for yourself treasure in heaven, where neither moth nor rust consumes and where thieves do not break in and steal.

(**Man** *enters carrying treasure box and places it on the altar.* **Friend** *enters at back of congregation and waves,* **Man** *waves back.*

Woman *tries to wave but is distracted by the need to hold onto treasure.*)

For where your treasure is, there will your heart be also.

(**Thief** *creeps off.* **Man** *and* **Woman** *face audience.* **Woman** *having placed treasure off stage.*)

The eye is the lamp of the body, so if your eye is sound your whole body will be full of light; but if the eye is not sound your whole body will be full of darkness.,

(**Woman** *looking carefully, finds her way over an area of rough and rocky ground.* **Man**, *with his hands over his eyes, attempts to follow.* **Woman** *tries to signal when he is about to stumble, but he trips anyway and almost falls headlong.*)

If the light in you is darkness, how great is the darkness. You are the light of the world. You are the city set on a hill that cannot be hid.

(**Woman** *points to light in the distance high up.* **Man** *following the direction stares at the light also.* **Friend** *enters the stage area and similarly begins to stare.*)

Let your light so shine before men that they may see your good works and glorify your father who is in heaven.

(*All characters freeze, still pointing to the light.*)

THE JORDAN BANK

A group drama based on Matthew 3:13-17.

Characters: News Reporter, John the Baptist, three to five People.

Costumes: Not essential, though biblical costume can be used.

Props: Microphone for News Reporter. If the church has a p.a. system use a live microphone on a long lead. This will enable News Reporter to speak excitedly but not loudly.
Notes: Action and commentary are simultaneous.

(**News Reporter** *is onstage*)

News Reporter:
Here we are, viewers, on the banks of the River Jordan, east of Jerusalem. As you can see, John the Baptist is busy again today, baptising repentant sinners in the waters of the Jordan.

(*Enter* **John** *followed by* **People**.)

News Reporter:
The crowds have been gathering throughout the morning. The first ones have been here since dawn. It is being said here that this is one of the important religious events of our time; that John is a prophet of Jahweh.

(*One of* **People** *steps forward, speaks to* **John**, *then with* **John** *assisting, bends as if being ducked under water.*)

News Reporter:
There are others who are more sceptical about this young man. It is rumoured that he eats locusts and wild honey and lives rough in the desert, like an outcast. This, it is being said by the experts, is not the way God sends his prophets.

(**John** *baptises two or more* **People**.)

News Reporter:
Ladies and gentlemen, something seems to be happening. A man has stepped forward and John is talking to him but he is not baptising him. They are still talking. John looks as if he is not wanting to baptise this man. But now I see that he going ahead.

(*One of* **People** *talks to* **John** *who shakes his head and remonstrates.*
Then **John** *goes ahead with baptising the person.*)

News Reporter:
There is some disturbance in the crowd, the people are looking up. So is John the Baptist. Ladies and Gentlemen

John the Baptist seems to be listening to a voice from the clouds. And those people nearby can see something in the sky.

(**People** *nudge one another and look up.* **John** *looks up with surprise. The baptised person also looks up.* **People** *point up into the sky.*)

(*Pause as* **News Reporter** *moves closer to* **People**, *whispers to one momentarily, then moves back towards congregation to speak.*)

News Reporter:

Well, ladies and gentlemen, you must judge for yourselves. You too have been here, courtesy of our television company, and saw on your screens what has happened today. The man John the Baptist reputedly heard the voice of God speaking to him from the clouds and bystanders report seeing a dove descending to land on the baptised man. That is all we have to report to you today, viewers, I will return you to the studio for the rest of the news. This is Jane/John Green reporting from the banks of the Jordan.

(*Exit All Characters*).

CHAPTER SEVEN: Bible Stories: with Puppets

Puppet plays may be used in church at any time that a dramatic presentation is considered. Present a story that is a set Bible reading, or one that reflects the content of the sermon, such as a modern parable or everyday drama.

Why use puppets?

Puppets are very quickly alive. The illusion that they are living and communicating very rapidly draws the audience under their spell. Even the simplest puppet play can hold attention if crisply presented.

Drama is a fairly exposing activity for the actors. Many shy participants are unable to get far enough beyond their fear of being watched to enter into the role and gain from the experience. Yet many shy people will engage in becoming puppeteers, making a character come alive through a puppet. Perhaps they are separate enough from the puppet that, if there is laughter, somehow it is at the puppet, not at the invisible puppeteer.

Encourage adults and children to work together with puppets. Often the adults will be too shy without the children among them. The creativity that is expressed, as mixed age groups work together on such a project, enhances friendship and a sense of belonging, a sense of equality and brings lots of fun and laughter.

How to use puppets

Since there are many skills to be grasped in being a puppeteer, it is helpful to use a prepared script. If the members in your group are not yet able to read, use a script that is a clear narrative so the puppets can respond to the ongoing telling of the story, acting their part appropriately. Alternatively, the non-readers may take non-speaking parts. If readers are using a script, their words ought to be fully memorised, as it is extremely difficult to operate a puppet at arm's length, while reading a wobbling sheet of paper and kneeling on the floor.

The narrative method can be quick to prepare, therefore doubly useful for young children and mixed-age groups. The following is the method I use frequently for introducing puppets, then immediately developing a short presentation with a narrative.

1. Read the story for the group who will take part.

2. Hand out puppets according to the number of characters needed for the story.

3. All players 'rehearse,' finding ways for the puppets to show:
   feelings:—sadness, anger, joyfulness/happiness
   actions:—saying hello, shaking hands with each other, pointing the way, walking, sleeping, eating, picking up a prop, sitting.
   directions:—enter, exit, walking towards left and right.

4. Choose characters and walk through the story, including all the necessary actions and directions.

5. Make a puppet stage, using a curtain or blanket over a string, held across the playing area.

6. Read the story to congregation with puppets acting it out.

For a play with spoken parts, there are the following stages for rehearsal:

1. Read the story for the group who will take part.

2. Hand out puppets according to the number of characters needed for the story.

3. All players rehearse, finding ways for the puppets to act:
   feelings—sadness, anger, joyfulness/happiness
   actions—saying hello, shaking hands, pointing the way, walking, sleeping, eating, picking up a prop, sitting.
   directions—enter, exit, walking towards left and right.
   Add any additional actions that would be useful to your script.

4. Choose characters and 'walk through' story, including all the necessary actions and directions.

5. Read through the scripted lines taking appropriate parts, with the puppeteers still holding their puppets.

6. Now allow time for memorising the parts.

7. Run through the play with puppets in action for the puppeteers to bring together the lines and good clear actions. At first the actions may be ineffective as the puppeteers are distracted by the need to remember the words. This is the reason for experimenting with the actions in steps 3 and 4.

   Rehearse a number of times, as needed by the group.

8. Add any necessary trimmings, such as props and scenery.

9. Prepare a stage and present the play.

Performance

The nature of the event in which the performance fits will determine the length and type of presentation. Roughly, the smaller the audience and the more sympathetic it is, the less polished the performance need be. If however you plan to present your puppets to a big crowd on a special occasion, such as a festival service, spend time creating a sense of occasion, building up the atmosphere. Then both audience and players will be excited before the presentation happens and will enjoy it more. Consider:
- adding well-made props that are familiar to the puppeteers. Make them of papier maché or play dough.
- using special lighting, putting put the audience in semidarkness with the stage area brighter. Light should be in front of the puppets, between them and the audience, preferably coming both from above and below so the shadows are not too strong. Never have light behind the puppets.

Making puppets

Glove puppets can be home made. Draw around the hand of the puppeteer onto paper. In transferring this onto cloth, add at least an inch all round before drawing the seam line and make the two halves symmetrical, so the puppet can be used with either hand. Make the length sufficient to go well over the wrist; the audience don't want the illusion broken by the sudden emergence of a sleeve.

A sock can make an ideal basis for a caterpillar or creepy creature. Add a couple of buttons for eyes. You may wish also to fix a tongue inside its mouth.

Making props

Play Dough: Mix together one cup of flour, half a cup of salt and enough water to mix these to a stiff paste. Knead the dough briefly in flour to remove any stickiness. Mould the dough into small props and dry them out on a sunny window ledge, over a radiator or in a very low oven. Once hard, play dough can be painted and varnished.

Papier mache can be used for larger and less fragile props. These can then be painted and varnished and are lighter and less breakable than those made of play dough.

The Stage

It is possible to use a box-like stage and puppet theatre as in the traditional Punch and Judy shows. However these can be quite limiting. Only two puppeteers can get inside, at the most, and movement is restricted.

A longer stage front may be constructed with cloth hung over a string (I use a long piece of furnishing hessian). This is both quick and easy. Scenery can be hung on a wall behind the puppets if necessary.

I once used a long piece of heavy striped canvas from a marquee. This was hung across a corner of the room, floor to ceiling, and a hole was cut out of it for the 'stage'. Several people at a time could get behind this screen with their puppets.

A roll of corrugated card of up to four feet width may be unrolled for the puppeteers to kneel behind. The scenery may then be pinned to the front.

See References for suppliers of glove puppets and of corrugated card.

THE FIVE THOUSAND

A narration for use with puppets, based on Matthew 14:13-23a.

Characters: Jesus, several Disciples, several people for a Crowd, Reader.

Props: Fish and bread cut from card. For biblical puppets — see information in Celebration Screenprint in References.

The playing area should be considered in several sections, so the puppeteers do not have to cross in front of each other. Jesus is to the left, the Disciples in the middle and the Crowd to the right.

Reader:
Jesus had received the news
(*Enter* **Jesus** *walking slowly with head bowed*)
That his friend John was dead.
Sadly, he went across the sea
To pray to his Father in heaven.

When the people saw that Jesus left,
(*Enter* **Crowd**)
Though he hoped to be alone,

They set out to follow on his path
(*Walk facing* **Jesus**' *direction*)
From all the local towns.

They walked along the lakeside
Where seagulls dipped and soared
And by remote and barren hills
(**Crowd** *sits down*)
They sat upon the shore.

Jesus saw them waiting there,
(**Jesus** *looks up*)
His heart went out to them.
He healed the sick they'd brought to him
(*Various* **Crowd** *come forward,* **Jesus** *touches their heads*)
And taught of his Father in heaven.

By and by the summer sun
Sank slowly in the west,
Still Jesus talked and healed the crowds:
(*Enter* **Disciples**)
The disciples were concerned:

"This is a very lonely place
And the sun is nearly set.
(**Disciples** *point to setting sun*)
Send these folk to the local towns
To see what food they can get."

Jesus looked up at the crowds
Who sat so patiently there

(*Shakes head, 'No' then points to* **Disciples**)
"No. They need not go away.
You find food somewhere."

The disciples were really taken aback
"But we have nothing to give.
(**Disciples** *hold up loaves and fishes*)
A boy has brought five barley loaves
And two small Galilee fish."

Jesus said, "Bring them to me.
And all of you crowds sit down."
(**Disciples** *bring food and hand it to Jesus*)
The disciples handed the food to him
And watched him with the crowd.

Jesus took the loaves and fish
Looked to God and gave him thanks
(*Holds up loaves and fish*)
And having blessed them, broke them up;
A miracle in his hands.

The disciples turned to the patient crowds
(*Pass loaves and fish along line of* **Disciples** *and* **Crowd**)
With ample fish and bread,
They handed supper out to them
Till everyone was fed.

The leftovers were collected till
Twelve baskets were filled up.
Five thousand people were fed that day

People old and young.

Finally the crowd dispersed,
(*Exit* **Crowd**)
The disciples sailed away.
(*Exit* **Disciples**)
Jesus set out into the hills,
(**Jesus** *turns and bows head, hands together*)
To be alone and pray.

THE GOOD SAMARITAN

A narration for use with puppets, based on Luke 10:25-37.

Characters: Reader, Merchant, Robbers, Priest, Levite, Samaritan, Donkey, Innkeeper

Props: Puppets, clubs for Robbers

Sound Effects: Whistling, groans

Scenery: Boulders by a wayside, over which the Robbers peer.

A simple inn may be shown at one side of the stage or on a back drop.

Reader:
>The road that led to Jericho
>From Jerusalem to the north
>Went narrow ways through rocky hills
>Winding on its course.

Along this road there travelled
One day, a merchant man;
(*Enter* **Merchant**, *walking*)
He had goods to sell on the market
Before he went back home.

He wondered as he journeyed
How much money he would make,
(*Sound of whistling*)
But though he had a heavy load
He dare not take a break;
(*Look around furtively*)
He'd heard that danger lurked this way
He hurried just in case.
(**Merchant** *walks faster*)

Aha, just down the dusty road
Someone looked about.
(*One* **Robber** *face peers out*)
A robber band was soon alert
Ready to jump out.

Thieves leapt upon the merchant
(**Robbers** *leap out and beat up* **Merchant**)
They knocked him to the ground;
They beat him with their wicked clubs
They stole his goods and ran.
(**Robbers** *exit*)

There by the side of the narrow road
The injured merchant lay;

(**Merchant** *lying, moves slightly and groans*)
>And the shadows grew much longer
>With the passing of the day.

>This pitiful man lay just like dead
>There wasn't too much hope,
>Unless some passing traveller
>Soon came and offered help.

>Some footsteps crunched upon the stones
(*Enter* **Priest**, *walking*)
>A priest was coming here;
>Now such a man would surely help,
>The footsteps drew quite near.

(**Priest** *looks at* **Merchant**)

>But that priest seemed rather busy
>He wanted to get to prayer;
(**Priest** *walks hurriedly and exits*)
>So he hurried past the merchant as if
>He hadn't seen him there.

>Now there came another man
(*Enter* **Levite** *walking*)
>Along the darkening road;
>He was a man who helped the priests,
>You could tell it by his clothes.

>But when he saw the merchant
(**Levite** *sees* **Merchant**, *jumps back, shocked*)
>He was really taken aback

>But did he help? Oh dear me, no;
>Perhaps he felt too shocked.
(**Levite** *hurries off*)

>There was no hope for the merchant now,
>Lying by the road.
(**Merchant** *turns over and groans loudly*)
>No one passed; not one who'd help;
>Now no one heard him moan.

>But then at last a new sound came,
>The tap of donkey hooves,
(*Enter* **Samaritan**, *walking and leading* **Donkey**)
>But this was only a Samaritan
>Who was hated by the Jews.

>But look at this, he's going to stop,
>To help the wounded man.

(**Samaritan** *stops, bends over* **Merchant**, *lifts him to lie over* **Donkey's** *back*)
>He cleaned the cuts, and helped him up
>Onto the donkey's back.

>They travelled slowly till they came
(**Donkey** *and* **Merchant** *walk slowly towards inn*)
>To a welcome wayside inn.
(*Enter* **Innkeeper**, *lifts* **Samaritan** *off* **Donkey** *and lays him down*)
>They tucked the merchant into bed
>And took good care of him.

TO DAVID'S TOWN

This narration is for a Christmas play. Alternatively, it may be used as a drama with congregation following an Action Leader.

Characters: Reader, Caesar, Joseph, Soldiers, Mary, Donkey, People, Camels, Innkeeper, Stable Animals, Baby, 2 or 3 Angels, Shepherds, Wise Men

Props: Parcel, gifts, biblical puppets (see References for suppliers)

Costumes: Crowns for Caesar and for Wise Men. Add wings for angels - these may be pinned onto the puppets.

For the stage: Since so many characters are involved in this Christmas story, EITHER use a very wide stage, allowing each group of characters its own part of the stage. In this case each puppet may be operated by a different person. For example, Caesar and Soldiers are far left, Mary and Joseph are centre and Wise Men are far right. OR 3 to 4 people could present different characters in turn.

Rehearsal: Follow the plan on page 51

Directions in *italic* give key movement of puppets, more may be added.

Reader:
'Twas many, many years ago,
(**Caesar** *enters, bows*)
When Caesar ruled the world,

Joseph was a carpenter,
In Nazareth he worked.

Caesar wanted to count up
(**Caesar** *points at audience*)
All the people that he ruled,
So soldiers marched to all the towns
(**Soldiers** *enter, point offstage right*)
Said, "All of you, go home!"

(**Caesar** *and* **Soldiers** *exit.* **Mary, Joseph** *and* **Donkey** *enter*)

Joseph had to set off south
(*load parcel on* **Donkey**)
To ancient Bethlehem.
(**Mary, Joseph** *and* **Donkey** *walk*)
Mary, his wife, was pregnant
But she packed her things and came.

(**Mary, Joseph**, *and* **Donkey** *walk slowly along*)

Mary and Joseph trudged along
Down winding, dusty roads,
With crowds of other people who
Must go to David's town.

(**People** *enter and chat to each other, shaking hands*)

At last they came to Bethlehem
(**People** *bump each other*)
But people filled the roads,
With barging camels and busy stalls

There was scarcely room to move.

(*Exit* **People**)

'What's to be done?' thought Joseph,
(**Joseph** *looks around*)
'Where will all these people stay?
And what will I find for Mary and I,
(*Arm around* **Mary**)
Before the end of the day?'

All of the inns were booked right up;
(**Joseph** *knocks on doors*)
Whatever space could they get?
Till a friendly innkeeper helpfully said,
(**Innkeeper** *points way*)
'I've got a stable to let.'

(*Enter* **Stable Animals**)

So in among the animals
Out at the back of the inn,
(**Mary** *and* **Joseph** *sleep*)
Mary and Joseph found a place
That was dry and very warm.

By and by it came the time
(**Mary** *picks up* **Baby**)
When Mary's babe was born.
So she laid him in the manger
While all the beasts looked on.

(*Enter* **Angels**, *who stand away from stable*)

Angels sang in the starry sky
(**Angels** *dance very lightly*)
Proclaiming Jesus birth.
(**Angels** *point up*)
'Glory be to God on high
And peace to all on earth.'

(*Enter* **Shepherds** *with* **Lambs** *and look towards* **Mary** *and* **Joseph**)

Shepherds watched their sheep that night
Till they heard the angels sing.
They left their flocks, to the stable ran,
To worship the new-born King.
(**Shepherds** *bow*)

(*Enter* **Wise Men** *with* **Camel**, *move slowly*)

A stately eastern caravan
Came near to Bethlehem,
Three wise men left their camels and
(**Wise Men** *give gifts*)
To Jesus they bowed down.
(**Wise Men** *bow down*)

Sermons are the interpretation of God's word in the present situation. In them much valuable teaching may be given by experts, those who have studied theology and understand the culture and theology of biblical times and the Christian heritage. But when looking at the meaning of the word for the present day it will be more effective in the lives of the people if they are able to struggle for themselves to find the meaning. It is not possible for one person to tell a church how to live out the gospel. The people in their continuing encounter with God will be able to say what the word means for their daily lives.

Such a process may be facilitated by a leader asking for comments in response to a question, "What is God saying to us about this?" and people may talk very honestly about the application of the word. However, making the word visual and meaningful for everyday life can effectively be done with the addition of drama and other visual forms of presentation, especially those in which the people may participate and to which they can contribute in ideas and workmanship.

Presentation

Whenever one person is going to present the sermon as a talk, consider carefully the content and the best form of communication. What is God saying to the church today? Look at the historical, theological and doctrinal context and content of the day's readings. Discover the key point or relevance from among the many interesting aspects and summarise those in one sentence! Keep all the other aspects in mind. If possible, in planning the actual communication find biblical, personal and local stories that illustrate this key point. Use the various other points to support the sermon and theme by using them in banners, songs and movement in the service. For fuller consideration of this thematic planning see Chapter 14.

Since it is so helpful for members of the congregation to discuss and work with the meaning of the theme, have either a small group or the larger congregation plan a modern parable to illustrate the importance of the theme for them. Together create a modern parable or update a biblical one to explain what the Scriptures have to say to the church today. In this section "The Mustard Tree that Grew" and "The Compost Heap" are examples of parables old and new.

Make a banner in preparation for the theme of a service and of the preaching. A banner may also use a 'catch phrase' from the sermon and keep that phrase visually before people.

Advent can be a good time to break into groups and let the congregation make specific and real plans for the preparation for the coming of the Lord. That will facilitate the church's taking on a greater element of worship in what can be a very commercial and ungodly event. They could prepare a festive and joyous, eventful, yet Christ-centred Christmas.

GLORY

A reading with actions, telling of the revelation of God's glory in creation.

Characters: Two Readers, Puppeteer

Props: Paper cut-out balloon, balloon, caterpillar puppet: made from a sock with 2 large button eyes, butterfly wings: made of paper with elastic loops on the underside for puppeteer to slide on over the caterpillar, paper grass and flowers.

The grass and flowers are taped to the pulpit; when the caterpillar appears it eats the flowers, pulling them off one at a time and 'munching' them (by screwing them up).

Readers: practise leading slowly and clearly with slight pauses to allow each word to sink in.

1: Glory
2: The weight of the presence of God
1: Bigness
2: Strength
1: Gentleness
2: Compassion
1: Radiance
2: Brightness
1: Greatness
2: Power.

1: Moses saw the glory of God on the earth,
2: The voice that spoke from the burning bush.

1: John saw God's glory in Jesus Christ,
2: Saw and touched, felt and knew.

1: And for us
1,2: Where is God's glory?

1: Sometimes we have symbols like a paper balloon

(*holds up paper balloon*)

2: (*blowing up balloon and releasing it*)
Sometimes we have the real thing.

1: There are many symbols of God's glory on the earth
2: A candle
1: A cross
2: A dove
1: A rainbow
2: A star.

1: Then there is around us God's glory,
2: To see and touch, to know and tell.

1,2: Where is God's glory?

1: One day there was a boy named Ian who found a caterpillar (*enter* **Caterpillar**) crawling on a leaf. He kept the caterpillar in a matchbox and let it out to eat. He liked the caterpillar very much and called it Charlie, but Charlie never spoke. One day Ian opened the matchbox and found that Charlie Caterpillar had turned hard and dry, (**Caterpillar** *falls onto its back*). He wouldn't eat anything and he still wouldn't answer when Ian spoke to him. Very sadly Ian took the matchbox out into the garden and tipped Charlie onto the ground. (**Caterpillar** *falls out of sight, with bang on side of pulpit*).
On Saturday morning, when there wasn't any school, Ian played in the garden. He was whistling

and swinging when he saw (enter **Butterfly**) a butterfly that fluttered closer and closer.

Suddenly Ian stopped whistling and swinging, and shouted for joy. Charlie was a butterfly! Ian could tell it was Charlie because the butterfly had a very particular look in his eye.

2: The glory of God makes the caterpillar eat.
1: The glory of God makes the chrysalis sleep.
2: The glory of God makes the butterfly fly.
1: The weight of God's presence is life.

2: Jesus said to his Father: The glory which you have given me I have given them, that they may be one as we are one.

1: Paul said: We are to live for the praise of his glory. To him be glory in the church and in Christ Jesus for ever and ever. Amen.

ONCE UPON A COMPOST HEAP

A group drama adapted from a story by members of the Community of Celebration, Woodland Park, Colorado.

Characters: Compost, Sun, two Clouds, Thunder, Lightning, Rain, Sunflower, Reader.

Props: Ragged brown robe for Compost, cardboard sun, paper clouds, large sheet of card to make thunder, silver paper or card flashes for Lightning.

Each character enters and exits appropriately as story unfolds. Sun, Sunflower, and Compost remain onstage throughout, Compost kneeling at the centre front of stage throughout till story requires him/her to stand, at which point Sunflower wilts to the floor. Sun lifts cardboard sun high when beaming. Sunflower should be instructed to fall over when Compost stands up.

Rain leads the congregation in making the rainstorm by imitating him in clapping first one finger, then 2, then 3, then 4, on the palm of the opposite hand to create sound of increasing fall of rain.

Narrator: Once there was a garden behind a house in a town.
It was a sunny garden, with a lawn for running on and borders where flowers grew. There was a vegetable patch too and the sun smiled as he shone down on the garden.
Not that the sun always shone. Sometimes great clouds would float across the sky, the thunder would roll and rumble and the rain would teem down. The plants drank thirstily as their roots sank further into the rich soil.
So God gave all sorts of weather to the garden by the house in the town.
Against a wall at the far end of the garden, far from the house, was a compost heap. Here the gardener put all sorts of scraps and plant bits, peelings and eggshells, everything that goes to make good rich fertiliser.
So we have a compost heap.
In the spring the gardener planted a new seed in the rich dark soil of the compost heap. It was a sunflower. The

sun shone and the rain fell and the little seed sprouted up growing taller and leafier, smiling up at the beaming sun.

Then one day the sun began to talk, to everyone who would listen. He grumbled about the rain that fell from the great dark clouds that drifted across his clear blue sky. It always interrupted just when he had got all the earth nicely warmed up.

Rain disagreed with this so she sent some fierce black clouds across the sky to argue with the sun, for if the sun had his way he would scorch up the poor sunflower and all the other plants.

The argument got really very heated so that thunder and lightning joined in, flashing and banging around the sky.

At last, compost could bear the argument no longer. He stood up sternly. (**Sunflower** *wilts*). If it weren't for him there would be nowhere for sunflower to put her roots while the sun shone and the rain fell. So after all was said and done he was the most important.

Then a hush fell. They all looked round, for poor sunflower now lay uprooted on the ground, her petals wilting and her leaves shrivelling.

Compost gathered up her roots and gently patted the soil around them. The sun shone warmly with an encouraging smile. Clouds dropped a soft refreshing drizzle and thunder and lightning hovered quietly on the horizon.

It was not long before sunflower struggled upright and smiled at her friends. She needed them all.

That was how God had made them, to work together.

THE MUSTARD TREE THAT GREW

A group drama based on Matthew 13:31-32.

The readings are from Matthew 13:31-32 and Psalm 84:1-4. John 12:1-7 may also be used.

Characters: Mustard Tree, Sparrow, Lord (can be offstage voice), Storyteller

Props: Twigs and leaves are scattered on the stage for the building of the nest.

Costumes: Both Mustard Tree and Sparrow should be costumed.

(*enter* **Mustard Tree**)

Mustard Tree: Good morning, good morning. It's time to rise and shine. Shake a leaf and brush the sleep from out of the twigs.
Hmm ... what a nice day.

Lord: Hello, Mustard Tree. I see you are in fine form and feeling well.

Mustard Tree: Yes, I'm really well, thank you. Look at these new shoots and this branch is growing well, it was a bit slow at first.

Lord: I'm glad to see what a fine mustard tree you've turned out to be. I like it when things turn out the way I intended them to be.

Mustard Tree: (*embarrassed*) Oh, do you really think so?

Lord: Have a good day, won't you? I'm sending the sun today, with a little breeze.

Mustard Tree: Just what I need for finishing off these leaves. Thank you. Goodbye.

Storyteller: And the sun shone and the wind blew. The leaves shimmered and fluttered as their colours grew richer in the warm sunlight.

(*Enter* **Sparrow**. *Goes to* **Mustard Tree** *and, taking twigs from the ground, begins to build a nest*.)

Mustard Tree: (*shaking branches*) What's going on there? What are you doing?

Sparrow: It's a nest, I'm building my nest here. It's that time of year now you know.

Mustard Tree: Time, my roots! Time has nothing to do with it! I'm very carefully shedding all those twigs because they're not good enough for a fine mustard tree like me. Why even the Lord was congratulating me this morning on what a fine mustard tree I am.

Sparrow: But I need these twigs for my nest to make it strong for my eggs and for the chicks when they hatch.

Mustard Tree: Chicks! On my branches! Oh no! They're so noisy and so messy. All those white spots on my clean branches. Really that would be just too much.

Sparrow: Please let me put my nest on your branch and make my home here?

Mustard Tree: But a nest would look so ugly just there, not at all pleasing to the eye. And chicks are so uncultured. Mustard seeds that grow into mustard trees are about the only kind of babies I'll have around, thank you. No birds here, I'm much too fine a mustard tree.

(*Exit* **Sparrow** *slowly and sadly, carrying the twigs*)

Lord: The kingdom of heaven is like a grain of mustard seed which a man took and sowed in his field; it is the smallest of the seeds, but when it has grown it is the greatest of shrubs and becomes a tree. So the birds of the air come and make nests in its branches.

(*Pause.* **Sparrow** *returns, clutching bunch of twigs and straw; carefully places twigs on a branch.* **Mustard Tree** *smiles*)

Storyteller:
How lovely is your house, O Lord of hosts.
My soul longs and faints for your courts;
My heart and my body sing for joy to the living God.
The sparrow has found a home at last,
The swallow a nest for its babies,
At your altars, O Lord of hosts,
My King and my God.
Blessed are those who dwell in your house always singing your praise.

BREAD FROM HEAVEN

Based on Exodus 16:11-18, Numbers 11:4-9, John 6:32-69

Characters: Readers 1—5

Readers: practise speaking out slowly and clearly, pausing slightly at the end of each line so the words can be taken in by the congregation.

1:　　And the Lord said
2:　　"Behold
3:　　I will rain bread from heaven
4:　　For you."
3:　　And when the dew was gone
　　　　There was manna
2:　　Like white hoar-frost
5:　　On the ground.

1:　　And the people said,
All:　(*random*) What is it? What is it?

4:　　It is the bread
3:　　That the Lord gave you
4:　　To eat.

1:　　And the people of Israel wept
5:　　Each at the door of his tent,
2:　　Oh, for some meat.
3:　　Remember the fish.
4:　　Where are the leeks?
5:　　Where are the melons?

All:　Where are the garlics and onions?
5:　　But there was nothing but manna to eat.

1:　　And many years passed
　　　　Till the Son of Man came
　　　　With another bread from heaven.
3:　　And Jesus said
2:　　"I am the bread of life.
4:　　Your fathers ate manna and died.
3:　　This is the bread that a man may eat
5:　　And not die.

2:　　And the bread which I give
3:　　For the life of the world
4:　　Is my flesh."
3:　　And many were angry,
2:　　Upset,
4:　　Offended.
1:　　(*sadly*) They turned, and followed no more.

TIME TO WAKE UP

A group reading accompanied by actions.

Characters: Readers 1 and 2, two assistants

During the first half of the reading from line five to line twenty four, Christmas symbols are hung from a washing line held across the front of the worship area. During lines twenty-nine to forty-four, remove items from the line, leaving only the candles. The two readers divide the spoken words as indicated, while assistants hang the symbols on the line.

Props: String, pegs, Christmas tree, pudding, tinsel, lights, parcels, candles, turkey, bottles. Most can be cut-out shapes, but some such as tinsel and lights may be real.

1: Time to wake up, it's Advent,
The coming of the King.
In ages old as prophets told,
It's time to prepare for him.

2: Aha! I know it's Christmas soon
All sorts of things to prepare;
I've been hiding secrets for ages now,
No one knows that they are there.

1: I bought a tree, a nylon one,
Very soon we'll have it up.

2: I've bought the frozen turkey,
Takes two days to thaw it out.

1: I've bought the cheer-filled bottles
To warm the cockles of our hearts.

2: And there's loads and loads of presents;
You have to, they're all part.

1: We'll light the Christmas candles
And have crackers at the feast;

2: I'll get the box with tinsel and lights;

The whole house will look a treat.

1: Make sure the telly's working
There's lots of special films,

2: And just in case, the video shop
Has lots we haven't seen.

(*Assistants freeze*)

1: When God prepared for Advent, he took
More than a thousand years,
Carefully to prepare the world
For his son who was coming here.

(*Begin removing symbols*)

2: He didn't send a rich man
All tinsel and bright lights;
He didn't come to entertain
But brought the gift of new life.

1: God prepared the way with ordinary folk
A carpenter and his wife;
And out in the desert a wild man preached
Of a peasant who'd bring a new life.

2: They didn't need a turkey,
Or a video in case they were bored,
They didn't look for trimmings or
For things they could hardly afford.

1: Jesus didn't come with riches
But to a stable stark and bare,

To humble folk with welcoming hearts,
The best that God could prepare.

2:   God won't be choosing rich men
During Advent-time this year;
He'll tell us ordinary working folk
To welcome Jesus here.

EXPECTATIONS

Characters: Readers 1—4. In selecting the readers, consider carefully who might best communicate the content of that section of the reading. For example Reader 2 would be an older man or woman.

Reader 1:

I'd waited for days.
I'd seen the package under the tree—just waiting.
I'd read the label and there was my name.
I dreamed and dreamed.
I knew it would be something just perfect.

I opened the parcel and said
"This is just what I've always wanted."

Oh dear. But now I've got it, do I really want it?
Or is it like other dreams that aren't quite so good when they come to life?

Why is the present so mundane,
When the future holds so much?

Reader 2:

Now I remember the real Christmas
We had when I was a child.
The sprouts, the sauce, the stuffing, the turkey,
And Dad carved.
We all sang carols and called 'Merry Christmas'
And it always snowed.

Reader 3:

But we've had all those this Christmas,
The food, the booze, the films,
We spent our cash and bought a lot,
Wasn't this Christmas real?

Reader 2:

This year the turkey was very small
And the sprouts were overdone,
The pudding was fair
But the sauce was scarce,
For all the people who'd come.

The kids weren't very happy
With all the gifts they'd got
In my young days
We got fruit and paints,
Not sweets and computer games.

No, everything's wrong with the present day,
The kids, the food, the pace.
I'll remember those Christmases long since gone
For those were better days.

Reader 4:

I want to take this Christmas
And give it to you.
Like a parcel unwrapped from glitter and cards,
I want to give this to you.

I want to give you Christmas food,
Not just turkey beautifully done;
I want to give you Christmas food:
Friendship, laughter, fun.

I want to give you Christmas light,
Not a tree soon empty and bare;
I want to give you Christmas light:
My friendship, attention, care.

THE LIGHT OF THE WORLD

A reading with congregational participation.

Characters: Reader

At the end of each verse the congregation join the Reader in repeating the last line. Rehearse this briefly before presentation, encouraging the congregation to reflect the emphasis as well as repeat the words.

Reader:

When Jesus came to Bethlehem
He was born in the manger hay.
He preached giving up riches and helping the poor,
And the rich men turned sadly away.

All:

And the rich men turned sadly away.

Reader:

When Jesus came to Bethlehem
He was worshipped by shepherds poor
He preached justice and mercy for everyone,
But the church men said, ''We're for the law.''

All:

But the church men said, ''We're for the law.''

Reader:

When Jesus came to Bethlehem
The angels sang ''Peace on earth.''
And the ordinary people said 'Praise to God'
When they heard the Good News of his birth.

All:

When they heard the good news of his birth.

Reader:

So Jesus comes to bring life today
He is coming, with light for the earth.
Are we prepared, we ordinary folk,
Shall we welcome the Light of the World?

All:

Shall we welcome the light of the world?

THE THIRD LITTLE PIGGY

by Alex Simons
© Copyright Alex Simons 1986. Used by permission.

A group drama.

Characters: Piggy, Narrator, Postman, Miss Piggy

Props: Rolled up architect's plans, phones, newspaper, chair

Narrator is onstage throughout and moves only to pick up the phone.

(**Piggy** *is seated onstage reading a newspaper*)

Narrator: Once upon a time there were three little piggies who had just moved into the neighbourhood. Each bought a plot of land on which to build a house. The first two little pigs threw together a couple of quick jobs, made of straw and sticks, branches and stuff. But the third little pig asked me if I would draw him up a plan. So I got out my drawing board and came up with a plan. I drew it out carefully, and sent it to him right away.

(*Enter* **Postman** *carrying plans which are handed to* **Piggy**)

Piggy: The plans have arrived. How exciting! (*looking over plans from all angles*) Well, I can't make this out. They look like the wrong ones to me. Much too big—I don't need all these rooms. And why would I want a house made of bricks? They're much too expensive, entirely unnecessary and a waste of time. I think these must be the wrong plans.

(**Piggy** *picks up phone*)

Narrator: (*while* **Piggy** *is dialling*) So I got a call from him the very day he got my plans.

(**Narrator** *picks up phone*)

Piggy: Hello, is that you? Well, I'm just phoning about the plans that came today. You sent me the wrong ones; I'll send them back, but can you send me the right ones straight away?

Narrator: Those are the right plans, Piggy.

Piggy: They can't be the right ones! The house is too big. It has too many rooms. It just won't do.

Narrator: I think you'll find that it's ideal.

Piggy: But you've designed a brick house that would take ages to build and I would like something quicker. I've got better things to do with my time and money than build a brick house.

Narrator: I'm sorry Piggy, it really is the best -

(**Piggy** *slams down the phone*)

Narrator: So he hung up on me. He spent the next couple of hours moping around the house. Then Miss Piggy arrived.

Miss Piggy: (*entering*) Hello, Piggy. What are you doing?

Piggy: I want to build a house, a really nice house. But he sent me these plans and they are all wrong. It makes me so cross. I wanted a nice little house—it could even be prefabricated for quick working—and he sent me plans for a brick house with so many rooms it will take forever to build and use all my money. It makes me really very angry!

Miss Piggy: But Piggy dear, leave those silly old plans and take me out for the evening. We could go to a quiet little bistro and perhaps dance together.

Piggy: I'm so sorry, Miss Piggy, but I must sort out these plans.

Miss Piggy: Oh, you just don't care about me do you? You only care about your silly old plans! (*exit stormily*)

Narrator: So off she went in a huff. Of course, Piggy thought it was all my fault. So he rang me up again.

Piggy: (*into phone*) Look, this has all gone too far. These plans are causing far too many problems. First, they were not suited to my ideas and now Miss Piggy has gone and left me. I am really very angry. I would have thought you could do better than this.

Narrator: Piggy, I am sorry you are so upset about the plans. I thought you really wanted plans from me and those are the best I can offer you. It's up to you whether you use my plans or not. You must decide.

Piggy: Harrumph! (*slamming down the phone*)

Narrator: (*While* **Piggy** *marches angrily backwards and forwards over the stage area, occasionally looking at the plans again*) This kind of wrangling went on for several weeks. Every now and then Piggy would get on the phone and go on at me about 'stupid' plans. I really wasn't sure he would ever use the plans I had sent him. But finally he came to a decision.

Piggy: (*halting centre stage and speaking to audience*) I suppose I had better follow his plans. He is supposed to know about building. (*exit* **Piggy**)

Narrator: And we all know which house it was that didn't blow down when the wolf came along huffing and puffing. And Piggy had enough rooms to put up the other two poor little piggies.

THE MOST PRECIOUS PEARL

A group drama based on Matthew 13:45-6.

Characters: Reader, David, Old Man, two or three Neighbours

Props: Tennis ball as pearl, bench for old man, several bags of gold

Costumes: Old Man wears a dark, hooded robe

Notes: David uses the entire stage area and church or hall for the search, including among the congregation and the seats. The bench for the Old Man's house should be clearly visible on the stage area.

(**David** *is lying in the sun, smiling contentedly at all the good things he owns*)

Reader:

It was a plain and sunny day,
And in a very ordinary way,
David was feeling quite satisfied
As he dreamed his life away.
He sat on the lawn in splendour cool,
By his pool of shining blue,
Thought of his camels, so sleek and brown,
And the racing camel that was new.

A restless mood came over him
As he lay there in the sun,
(*Turns uncomfortably from side to side*)
He'd felt like this so many times;
Was there something to be done?
(**David** *stands, stretches and paces up and down*)
A restless mood that niggled him,
Had him pacing up and down,
Wond'ring about what else he might seek,
Where an answer could be found.
(*Gestures that he has an idea*)

Not three days hence, about midday,
Our friend set out at speed,
(*Packs bags busily*)
With camels and food and water bags,
All the things a man could need
To search for the incredible something;
(*Sets out walking, leading camel*)
Who knows where his search might lead.

He crossed the sandy desert,
(*Coughs hoarsely, drinks thirstily*)
As the scorching sun beat down,
It made him dry and choking,
This endless dusty ground.
He climbed up mountains that reached the sky
And peered from the very top.
(*Climbs hand over hand, shielding his eyes peers into the distance*)
He crossed deep valleys and dangerous ravines
(*Leaps a wide ravine*)
On a journey that would never stop
Till he found that incredible something
(*Looking around to check bearings*)
That was somewhere to be found.

He braved thick jungles with tigers and snakes;
It was muggy and steaming and grim.
(*Fights his way through jungle undergrowth*)
There were nasty creepers that snaked around,
Maybe this was the end of him.
But intrepid he continued
On a dry and hazy plain;
His camels got tired and then gave up;
(*Waves wearily to camels and walks on*)
So he trudged on alone.

The Great Wall of China came into sight
(*Peers into distance*)
With a town and market stalls,

(**Neighbours** *enter onto street*, **David** *links arms and dances
with them*)
    And our traveller danced to the strangest sounds
    Beneath those ancient walls.
    Before very long he was on his way;
(*Sets out again, trudging wearily*)
    He wouldn't give up, he'd go on,
    He'd go on and on to the end of the road,
    He'd go on and on and on.

    It seemed that he must be right at the end,
(*Halts, looks around*)
    At the end of the world that is,
(*Spots* **Old Man's** *house and walks over to it*)
    When he spied a sight on a distant hill,
    An old and ancient house,
    With tree-lined drive and rustic hedge,
    An old-fashioned wrought-iron gate.
    As he drew near he saw, by the door,
(*Enter* **Old Man** *sits on bench*)
    A happy old gentleman sat.

    Here was the man with the secret of life
    Here was a man who would know
(**David** *shakes hands with* **Old Man** *and sits beside him*)
    Why the traveller had come so far
    And where else he might go.
    The old man opened a box at this side,
(**Old Man** *pulls pearl from pocket*)
    A battered leather case,

    Held out his treasure, on outstretched palm,
(**David** *stares incredulously*)
    A pearl of incredible size.

    David stood speechless, filled with awe,
    He'd searched and now it was found,
    The most precious thing that he'd ever seen,
    For this he'd give all that he owned
(*Counts on his fingers, searches his pockets*)
    Just to have in his hand the incredible pearl;
    So here was the end of his search.

    He promised the man his camels sleek,
    He'd deliver them right away;
(*Crosses stage and sells his belongings to* **Neighbours**, *haggling
over prices*)
    Sold his house, his pool and his shining Porsche
    All his treasure was sold that day.
    All that he owned was turned into gold;
    All that five bags could hold.

    He returned to the house on the distant hill,
    Where the old man sat by the door,
    And gave him the money, five bags of gold,
(*Hands over heavy bags of gold*)
    He would gladly have given him more.
(*Receives pearl*)
    It's long and hard just to decide
(*exit* **Old Man**)
    What in the world is most precious to you,
(**David** *stands staring at pearl*)

But when you find the kingdom of God
That's how precious will be the view.
And when you see it, give all that you have,
That's the price of the kingdom for you.

© Copyright Celebration Services (International) Ltd., 1977.
Used by permission.

THE EGG AND THE CHICK

Characters: Mary, Christopher, John

Props: Small boxes containing fluffy chicks

(*Enter* **Mary** *stroking and fussing over the chick in her hand*)

Mary: (*on reaching the stage area*) Look at this. Look what I've got. I kept an egg in the airing cupboard; see, I've got a chick now.
I had to leave it a long time in a box of cotton wool, and today it broke its shell and got out.
Isn't it beautiful and fluffy and soft.

(*Enter* **Christopher**)

Mary: Christopher! Look! My egg hatched and I've got a baby chick now.

Christopher: Oh, you haven't!

Mary: I have, y'know. Come and look.

(**Christopher** *crosses the stage and peers closely*)

Christopher: Hmm. It looks like one. Where did you get it?

Mary: It was in my box in the airing cupboard. It hatched out. The shell is still there.

Christopher: It looks too big to fit in that egg you had.

Mary: Come with me and I'll show you.

(*Exit* **Mary** *and* **Christopher**.)

(*Pause, then they re-enter.*)

Mary: See, I told you it had hatched.

Christopher: It doesn't look possible, does it?

Mary: No. But before it fluffed out its feathers it was quite skinny and small.

(*Enter* **John**)

Christopher: John, Mary's egg has hatched and she's got a chick.

John: Huh. Where did you get the chick, Mary.

Mary: It hatched in the airing cupboard.

John: (*scornfully*) Huh!

Mary: You don't believe me, do you?

John: No, I don't. You just got your mum to buy you a chick so it would look like the egg had hatched.

Mary: I did not!

John: I bet you did!

Mary: Oh… you're horrible. I didn't.

Christopher: What happened to your egg, John?

John: Nothing.

Christopher: Mary's egg hatched, yours might too.

John: Hers didn't. And mine won't.

Christopher: Well, get yours and look.

John: You can get it if you want to. It hasn't done anything.

Christopher: I will get it. I want to see.

(**Christopher** *exits and re-enters carrying a small box with cotton wool just showing at the edge*)

Christopher: Here it is.

John: Look, nothing's happened. It's just a rotten old egg.

Christopher: What's that little bump on it?

Mary: It's moving, I can see it moving.

Christopher: It's breaking the shell from the inside. It's hatching. John, your egg is hatching.

John: (*watching intently*) Hmm … it is.

Mary: (*reaching to take the box*) Let me see.

John: Leave it alone, it's my chick.

Christopher: Look it broke the shell right open.

Mary: It's getting out! It's getting out.

John: Be careful, you lot, that's my chick. (*Lifts chick from box so audience can see*) Hey listen, I'm going to show my mum. I bet she'll never believe it.

(*Exit* **John** *followed by* **Mary** *and* **Christopher**.)

72

CHAPTER NINE: Prayer

When God's people gather for a worship service they are gathering primarily to praise God and offer their love in response to his love. Through this, the people come to a common awareness of his relationship to them, his greatness, his love, his omnipotence, his majesty, and his compassion. Each service contains times of prayer and supplication, times when the people speak to God. The praise incorporates thanksgiving, in words as well as music. The focus of praying that presents the concerns of the people to God is however more particularly in the Confession and in the Intercessions.

Confession is an integral part of a congregation coming together into the presence of God, for in the confession the people acknowledge that they are failing to express the fullness of what it means to be the body of Christ on the earth. Confession in the liturgy is not only a time for individuals to confess the times they recollect having sinned in the last week, but also to acknowledge that imperfection is their nature and it is only by the redemption of Christ that they enter into the presence of God. The church is in much the same place as Isaiah who came into the presence of God where it was necessary for one of the seraphim to take a burning coal to touch Isaiah's lips; for Isaiah saw himself to be "a man of unclean lips, and ...(dwelling) in the midst of a people of unclean lips."

God is present and ready to listen to the requests of his people. The church as a people may present their concerns to him. There may be individuals to pray for, needs in the world, mission and work.

For many congregations, it is helpful to the growth of members to find a way for individuals to present their own needs, in addition to those aspects of intercession that represent the corporate concerns of the church, and so be affirmed in their own relationship to him. This may be especially true when young children are present. Participation in prayer helps the individual's becoming aware that God is listening to her prayers, along with the prayers of others present.

Often children have a directness that can bring deeper awareness of the real meaning of intercession. Children who are aware of the needs of others expect to do something to help, whether to send food to Ethiopia or clothing to those in a flood disaster. To intercede is to get practically involved; it is not to pass the news of the need onto God and then forget it. The Church is the body of Christ in the world, doing his work, so intercession is integrally linked to practical involvement. If the Church doesn't get involved in the solutions to the problems, then it is doing empty lip-service to the concept of intercession.

Leading a time of participatory prayer

While prayers may be spoken by one person on behalf of everyone else present, there are factors that would point to looking for new ways to present prayers that are more open to the participation of others. It is hard for one person to know the concerns of others present, even if he or she is aware of concerns that the church has together, through being at Council meetings. For the majority of the congregation to know that the prayers represent them individually as well as corporately, there should be opportunity to be active in speaking to God. Only some members, even among adults, will be confident to stand in front of everyone, or speak out from the pew where they sit. So the following methods offer ways to introduce participatory prayer into the service, ways in which everyone regardless of age or experience may take part:

Using an overhead projector or blackboard, the congregation can call out items to be written up: requests for the church, requests for the world, personal concerns, thanks. These are then presented in a summarising prayer said by one member.

One-sentence prayers may be spoken from among the congregation. Children, and those less experienced in speaking in front of a crowd, are slow to join in, though they will eventually, as two steps are necessary: to think what to say and how to say it. Suggest that those who are unsure of how to speak out their prayer, tell the person next to them and perhaps that person can say it for them. This often means that a nearby adult will present the child's concern.

The most effective participatory form of prayer time in all age worship has been prayers in pairs. Tell the congregation to form pairs with those near to them. Suggest that each pair talk for a minute about the things for which each has been concerned this week. Then tell all pairs to say two one-sentence prayers together: representing the concerns of both partners. The process, first of telling the pairs to talk to each other then telling them to pray together, is repeated for giving thanks to God. (This process enables people first to voice their concern and subsequently to put it into a prayer.) This may then be followed with an opportunity for members of the congregation to call out the names of people that they would specially like to mention to God for the coming week.

In this time the names, of members and local people who are sick or in need of help are offered.

After any of these more subjective presentations of prayer, it is still possible to present the more formal or traditional forms used in the liturgy, so corporately presenting concern for the world, the church and the sick.

Occasionally pictures or collages may be brought to illustrate prayer concerns. See the workshop in Chapter Eighteen.

CHAPTER TEN: Dance

Historically, folk dance was an expression of celebration of the major festivals such as harvest, the New Year, the summer solstice and other festivals and community celebrations. People's hopes and fears, grief and joy found expression in movement. Folk dance has not often been primarily for performance though a performer may take a lead for part of the dance. Folk dance is essentially inclusive of people of varying ages and types.

For the whole congregation to celebrate in dance, folk dance is an excellent basic form. Such dances come naturally, are easy to learn and many people have already had some experience of the steps.

Dance in Worship

Introducing folk dance into worship services takes careful preparation. The congregation should know how and why dance is an appropriate form of worship. Dance is fitted carefully into the order of the service and there is careful consideration of how to teach dances and develop a repertoire.

In preparing the congregation, consider the Old Testament references to dance in worship, as at the time of the rebuilding of the temple in Ezra and Nehemiah. The Jewish people today still seem to have more dance in their family lives and community celebrations than many of us would expect in our Western cultures. Such examples show us that dance is not inappropriate in worship; it may be that we are just not used to it. Before introducing dance to any service, prepare the congregation with teaching on the offering of the whole of ourselves in worship and on movement as an expression of worship.

Preparation

Folk dance can be readily rehearsed by a small group of mixed ages. A large group can be harder to organise and introduce without disruption in the worship service.

With the musicians who will play the song during the service, prepare and rehearse the dance. If you use a record or cassette to accompany the rehearsal, have at least one rehearsal with the musicians. A rehearsal will give you time to iron out discrepancies - the musicians may set a pace that is very different from the rehearsal and too fast for the dancers.

In the Service

Initially a folk dance can be introduced at a festival service when an exciting celebration is planned. Use the dance at the end of the service before or during the last hymn, but before the blessing. In this position, the excitement generated within the dance will not break the natural flow of the service.

As the church becomes more accustomed to group dances, the offertory is another good opportunity for the dance, as there is already movement and change of pace at this stage in the service. If this is the time at which you take up a money offering from the congregation you may, however, wish to have an offertory song with the collection after the dance, as the congregation will be distracted from the passing offertory plate by the sight of the dance.

Some simple dances, such as ''On Tiptoe'', which is included in this chapter, may fit thematically with the readings or sermon and in this case may be used after the readings, before the sermon.

Other particular songs, such as "Ho, Everyone" (SOLW 88), may be set with a simple folk dance that is part of the procession at the beginning or end of the service. In this case the customary folk dance patterns can be adapted.

Developing Dances

Look through the music books that your church uses regularly for songs that would be suitable for accompaniment with a dance. Work out the basic idea with a musician, guitarist or pianist accompanying your selected dance pattern to check your idea is feasible before a group begins to work on it.

Very simple dances, preferably circle dances, such as "Circassian Circle," are most suited. They also have the advantage of adapting to almost any even number of dancers. Some reels would also be fitting, though choose carefully that they are not too complicated for all ages to participate.

Folk dances are most readily learned by imitation. Teach the dance to a group of eight people, then tell each of them to take a new partner who has never done the dance before and repeat the dance. The new learners are helped by dancing with those who have learned already.

See Appendix for details of the English Folk Dance Society, as a source for books of folk dance steps.

On Tiptoe

by Margi Pulkingham
and Community of Celebration Children

Circle dance: 4-8 dancers (children and one leader)
Dance begins with verse 1, and the chorus follows each verse.

CHORUS:

And all creation's straining
(*Place hands on knees; walk with bent knees around circle clockwise.*)

on tiptoe just to see
(*Stand upright on tiptoes, shading eyes by placing right hand on forehead. peer to left and right.*)

The sons of God come into their own.
(*Join hands, skip clockwise around circle.*)

VERSE 1:

I walk with you my children,
(*Walk clockwise around circle.*)

Through valleys filled with gloom;
(*Continue walking, making a dip on 'valleys' by bending low and straightening up again.*)

In echoes of the starlight
(*Standing still, all lean to the right and cup right hand over right ear, listening.*)

And shadows of the moon.
(*Swing right arm downwards in sweeping motion, gesturing to indicate shadows on ground.*)

In the whispers of the nightwind
Are gentle words for you
(*Turn to face centre of circle, bend slightly at waist. Sway upper body from left to right and make soft whistling sounds.*)

To touch you and assure you
It's my world you're walking through.
(*Turn 180°, gesturing, with gentle sweep of right arm, to include audience. Continue turning, completing a full circle.*)

VERSE 2:

I made the mottled stickleback to hide in crystal streams.
(*Wide-eyed, bend from waist and point right hand toward imaginary fish to centre of circle.*)

The staring owl to scan the night,
(*Hand on hips and 'hoooooot!'*)

The candle's gentle beams;
(*Stand, with hands above head, palms together to form a candle flame.*)

I made the silly camel
To roam the desert sand,
 (Turn to left, place hands on waist of person in front, all bend at waist and walk, swaying.)

If life were filled with jewels
They'd line a rich man's purse.
 (With both hands, open a imaginary money bag. Peer inside with wide eyes and wide mouth.)

But you I made, my children, to walk and hold my hand(s).
 (Join hands, walk around circle clockwise)

But life is filled with water
That flows from depths of love.
 (Raise right hand high and slowly move an arm in a flowing figure-8 fashion.)

VERSE 3:

If life were filled with bubbles,
 (Stand still, holding right hand up in air, joining thumb and forefinger together to form 'bubbles'.)

It flows to fill your weariness
With blessings from above.
 (Continue figure-8 motion; on 'blessings' raise both arms above head and then slowly lower them to sides, wiggling fingers to suggest falling rain.)

They'd glisten and they'd burst;
 (On 'glisten' spread fingers wide; on 'burst' pop an imaginary bubble with forefinger.)
 (Note: Drawing of leader only is for clarity, but children follow leader as before.)

VERSE 4:

My love for you, my children, puts rainbows in your hand.
 (On 'rainbows' each extends arms above head, forming arc with hands.)

Born of clouded sorrows
In sunburst morning land;
(*Droop upper body to left, arms still circled above head. On 'sunburst' thrust arms apart while quickly standing upright, bright faced.*)

They arch above the smiling eyes
(*Bend over at waist, rest chin on hands linked together at fingers, palms down.*)

Where tears can still be seen,
(*On 'tears' tilt head to right pointing with forefinger of right hand to right eye.*)

And adorn with gentle trembling touch
The bride who is my own.
(*Turn 180°, gesturing with gentle sweep of both arms, to include audience. Continue turning, completing a full circle.*)

God is our Father

Copyright © 1983 Celebration
Used by permission

This is a dance that everyone can join. The actions can be led by one or two people (or as many as 4) standing at the front facing the congregation, encouraging them to join in. In addition, there can be a circle of dancers who do the same actions with slight modifications (noted in the directions below). The circle must be an even number of dancers, divided into partners—minimum of 8; maximum 14. This can be a festive dance of thanksgiving with the circle of dancers moving around the altar if there is space.

God is our Father
(*Slowly raise opened right hand up, palm up.*)

For he has made us his children,
(*Bring right arm down to join left arm in forming a ring, as though holding and rocking a baby.*)

Made Jesus our brother,
(Slowly raise opened left hand up, palm up.)

 And hand in hand we grow together as one.
(Clasp hands with the persons on either side of you, and swing clasped hands back and forth in time to the music.)

 Sing praise to the Lord
(1. In broad sweeping motion, raise hands above head, making a quick clap at chest height on the word 'praise', carrying on to complete the arc.)

 with tambourine*
(*Pretend right hand is a tambourine. Make a shaking motion with open hand as you lower it to your side, then raise it again. Repeat.)

(Actions by the asterisk* happen in the musical space **after** *the words.)*

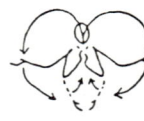 Sing praise to the Lord
(Repeat movement 1. as above.)

with clapping hands*
(*Clap hands to the rhythm below. The circle turn to their partners and clap in rhythm, first on their thighs, then their hands, then each other's hands.)

 Sing praise to the Lord
(Repeat movement 1.)

with dancing feet*
(*Starting with right foot, do three scottish 'set' steps, described below, first to the right, then left, then right.)

80

(a. Hop lightly onto right foot, bringing left close to right. Shift balance quickly to left, then back to right. R L R)

(b. Repeat, hopping to left L R L)

(c. Then repeat, hopping to right once more. R L R)

Sing praise to the Lord
(Repeat 1.)

with our voice, la la la la la la ...
(With rollocking motion, roll arms round and round, and backward and round and round again, going up and down, having fun with the movement.)

(The circle members do what is called a 'grand chain', weaving in and out of one another around the circle. They begin by turning to their partners, taking right hands, then moving past their partners on to the next person taking left hands and so on around the circle; they will meet their partners once but should carry on till they meet the second time; then stop in original positions. (If the 'la la la's' are not quite finished, the circle can join hands and swing them back and forth till the beginning phrase of the song comes round again.) The entire song is repeated once, and the final 'la la's' may be repeated one, two or three times. However, the number of repeats should be coordinated between the musicians and dancers so the circle know when they are finishing and can stop with their partners so the entire circle can raise their hands on the final 'la')*

Our Father

Copyright ©1979 Celebration
Used by permission

Congregational Hand Actions

These hand actions can be learned easily by following one or two people who have mastered them. Thus two people can learn the actions from the written instructions and rehearsal tape. They can teach the actions to the congregation by a simple talk-through of the 'Our Father' words, having the people mirror the leaders.

During the service, it is helpful to have one or two persons stand facing the congregation to lead the hand actions. (This person may be the celebrant.)

 Our Father
(Gently raise right arm.)

 in heaven,
(Gently raise left arm.)

 hallowed be your Name,
(Slowly lower arms and bow head.)

 your kingdom come,
(Thrust right arm upward with strength. Raise head.)

 your will be done,
(Thrust left arm upward with strength.)

 on earth as in
(Bring arms around in a large arc, continuing into next movement.)

 heaven.
(Raise hands in front of body to above head. Eyes follow hands up.)

 Give us today our daily bread.
(Bring hands together, cupped down in front of mouth. Bow head.)

 Forgive us our sins
(Cross arms over chest, palms open. Keep head bowed.)

 as we forgive those who sin against us.
(Reach out and take hands of those by you. Lift head.)

Save us from the time of trial,
(Do not bring us to the time of trial,)
(Lead us not into temptation,)
 (*With fists clenched, wrists crossed, move arms around slightly as in struggle.*)

and deliver us from evil.
(but deliver us from evil.)
 (*Release hands, uncrossing arms, bringing them up, around, and down to sides.*)

For the kingdom,
 (*Thrust right arm upward with strength.*)

the power,
 (*Thrust left arm upward with strength.*)

and the glory are yours, now and for ever.
 (*Bring arms together slightly above head, palms down. On 'glory' release hands and fingers upward in a little burst of energy. Slowly lower arms to sides in a gentle arc.*)

Amen.
 (*Lightly clasp hands together.*)

Come Go with Me to that Land
Adapted English Folk Dance

This dance requires four couples, arranged in a square; the man on the left, the woman on the right.
All steps are done with a simple running step as in English folk dances.
Music for the dance is found in *Fresh Sounds*, 78.

First Phrase: (Men/Women)

 (*Men begin the first verse; women begin the second. Continue the alteration throughout.*)

83

(Join right hands in centre of square to form a star. With running step, circle in clockwise direction. Partner stands in original position, claps in time to music.)

Well, come go with me to that land,
come go with me to that land,

Second Phrase: (Men/Women)

(Drop right hands, turn. Form star with left hands. Circle in anti-clockwise direction.)

come go with me to that land
where I'm bound.

Third Phrase: (Men/Women)

(Drop hands in centre. Join hands with partner, crossing hands in front. Promenade in anti-clockwise direction.)

Come go with me to that land,
come go with me to that land,

Fourth Phrase:

(Link right elbows with partner and turn in place. On last bar, stop turning and form square again, ready to begin next verse.)
to that land, to that land,
where I'm bound.

CHAPTER ELEVEN: Symbol and Movement

Symbols, in visual as well as dramatic forms, used in worship help teach God's character and remind people of their history. Many windows, banners and vestments have pictures on them of the dove, the rainbow, the lamb, the shepherd, a candle, a cross and many others, surrounding people with impressions of God's nature and his activity.

Symbolic actions are physical actions that have meaning in themselves, stronger than simply being reminders. Baptism and Eucharist are symbolic events that also have value in themselves. These are living symbols, carrying forward ways of being the Church over the centuries, fulfilling the word of Christ and acting on the present reality. They continue to bring God's word to his people. As sacraments, they are actions that are both signs of grace and a means by which God gives grace.

There are other actions in a service that may be symbolic while carrying real value in the lives of those enacting them. Many are thought of as optional ways of doing the service, and their significance to all age worship is that they communicate truth and the meaning and purpose of the church, without depending on words. In a service that is rich in such action, those present can, without necessarily understanding the language, begin to know and assimilate the life and focus of those present. In participation in such movement, the whole congregation is nurtured and enabled to be active in their faith. Words, whether as spoken praise or in teaching, then are complementary and explanatory of what the church does in faith. In acknowledging that all people learn through what they do, the movement and symbolic actions of worship have major significance in the growth of all ages.

In simplifying and shortening their customary worship service to accommodate all age worship, many churches drop the movements, which seem to them unnecessarily time consuming. However, for the nurture of the members, the movement is the most effective teacher. If shortness is a target, it is preferable to shorten the words!

Within the liturgical service there are many movements each of which symbolises, communicates and has real meaning. The solemnity of the procession at the beginning begins the service with a recognition of the uniqueness of the occasion, the significance and the importance of it to the participants. Those processing are visibly offering themselves to serve the congregation in leading the worship. Such a sense of occasion is not so readily communicated without the ceremony. The action communicates and incarnates the heart or will of the corporate gathering in its coming into a conscious focus on God. The procession is a call to worship that may then be affirmed in a spoken call that makes specific reference to the theme of the service.

The congregation stands for the reading of the gospel, the preacher coming down among the congregation to stand one of them, while reading the words. Acolytes carry candles to shine on the pages, an action that until recent years would have been necessary for the reader to see the pages clearly. The movements involved express the people's respect for the Scriptures and the preacher's identification with the congregation.

The movement of the congregation in standing, sitting and kneeling for various parts of the service also have inherent meaning. Standing at the beginning of the service marks the congregation's common identity with the procession and standing to sing or speak makes their praise more emphatic. The Pentecostal response of raising hands in praise, or the addition of actions to songs is a natural extension of that movement. Sitting is a more passive stance, one that signals listening and receiving. Kneeling is another active position, for prayer or for receiving the sacraments, when the congregation enacts its humility and its reverence for the word.

The collecting of money during the offertory hymn, and the carrying up of that money, at the same time as the bread and wine are carried forward and offered, enables the congregation actively and consciously to give the fruit of their labours to God. In past centuries, the bread and wine might have been made by members of the congregation—as the bread is today in the Orthodox tradition. Today, money is the more relevant sign of the people offering that for which they have worked. It would be relevant for children present to be making their own offering out of their pocket money at a rate equivalent to the offering their parents make, rather than putting in the plate coins popped into their hands by a parent moments before.

In the all age worship service, reconsider the liturgical form and the ways this is, or might be, expressed in movement, especially gestures in which the people may participate. On an ordinary Sunday, this may include little more than following in full the directions for movement that are given in the **Alternative Service Book** for Morning Prayer or the Eucharist. Look at the movements that the leaders may include, especially such actions as holding up the bread and wine when these are consecrated. Make the movement clearly visible to all.

On special occasions and on festivals, consider other movements. At the celebration of harvest have a liturgy for offering, when the people—adults and children—bring forward their gifts. During prayer for individual members of the congregation, have them come forward for anointing with oil or laying on of hands. When the whole congregation is to be prayed for, or a larger proportion, then have those in the pews pray and lay hands on one another.

When a particular movement of liturgical significance is taking place that would be unseen by most of the people present, consider how it might be made more visible. At one wedding I attended, between two adults who were youth and children's leaders in that church, there were many children present with whom the couple had close friendships. The priest on this occasion invited children to come to stand around him as he led the couple through the vows and the exchanging of rings. The friendship between leaders and children was acknowledged, as well as the action being made visible. The children, even the three-year-olds who went forward, respected the solemnity of the occasion and were quiet and still, watching with rapt concentration. They were active witnesses to something usually only seen by the priest or occasionally the camera. In some churches today, the baby who is being baptised is carried around among the congregation by the priest as an introduction to them of the person they are to receive among them as a member of the church.

The Christingle Service or the Christmas Toy Service are frequently rich in the symbolic movement of offering. At the Christingle Service, money is given and the decorated orange is received; the orange itself is wrapped in symbols of the Christian Church.

Other festivals may have relevant movement in them in ways that may be devised and developed by the worship leaders. Look among other Christian traditions for examples. A special Ash Wednesday service may involve each person coming forward to receive a cross marked in ash on her forehead as a sign of repentance. The ash itself is the residue from burning the Palm Crosses of the previous year.

New Symbolism

The charismatic renewal, which has challenged and changed the lives of many churches, has brought with it a demand that within the liturgy there be room for the gifts of the Spirit expressed through the congregation. This is in itself a sign of major change in the life of the contemporary Church, one that may be seen to be integral with the Church becoming the Church of the people, a reflection of John Tiller's report.[1] According to Paulo Freire[2] and Jurgen Moltmann,[3] having the right and opportunity to speak is a sign of power. The person who speaks and acts on the basis of his own speech is a powerful and self-determining person. In most of our churches, the right to speak has been retained by the priest or minister, and the people can only speak at his cue and under his direction. The result in the Church has been a false premise that the Church belongs to those in holy orders,

not to the people. For the Church to be the Church of the people, their right to initiate and speak words must find its place in the worship service.

Place will be found for at least some members of the congregation to interpret the Scriptures for today if they participate in creating modern parables in drama and mime. However, the time may be close when we may all expect to participate in the sermon through discussion of various kinds.

The inclusion of opportunity for the gifts of the Spirit to be expressed through the people is a symbolic and real acknowledgement and expression of their identity as the Church, through their right to speak on their own initiative. The placing of such opportunity at predetermined points integrates the spontaneity of charismatic worship into the liturgy and worship life of the Church. Making it thus an element of the structure of the liturgy confirms that all present are equal in the presence of God, all are together the Church and confirms the priesthood of all believers; the person who functions as priest does so as one of the people not as a member of a Church apart from the people. Thus we see the significance of symbolic action when the people are active individually and corporately.

The difficulties that may be feared, or that may actually arise, from inserting opportunity for the expression of the gifts of the Spirit reflect the change that is under way. Those who speak or offer those gifts may not be as aware as the designated worship leaders that for the sake of those present it is planned to finish the service at a specific time. Someone may launch into what is apparently a long and complicated prophetic word! Sometimes a disturbed person enjoys the opportunity to command attention and this is not a genuine prophecy! Such occasions are rare, and can be prepared for by those who teach, who can explain for the congregation the time schedule of the service and how those leading intend to keep to the intended schedule. If someone does get carried away with speaking, the leaders will recognise this to be inappropriate and not a genuine gift of the Spirit. It may be a word that the Spirit intends for that individual, not the whole gathering. In my experience genuine gifts of the Spirit in prophecy, tongues and interpretation in all age worship are concise and to the point. The Spirit knows the nature of the gathering.

Some worship leaders and ministers may fear that to include a time in the service when the gifts of the Spirit are spontaneously offered will result in their losing control of the service—and in the best possible sense, they will! As the leaders are accepted and trusted, their discernment will be accepted by the congregation if they appear to cut short such time. The gift of leadership among the people is recognised.

Notes

1. *A Strategy for the Church's Ministry*, John Tiller, CIO Publishing 1983.

2. *Pedagogy of the Oppressed*, Paulo Freire, Seabury.

3. *Power of the Powerless*, Jurgen Moltmann.

CHAPTER TWELVE: Liturgy

Liturgy that enables all the congregation to participate affirms everyone as an active participant in the statements that they make together; and the Church in recent years has looked for the people to be active members of the Church and more active in worship.

Liturgy gives a structure in which all can take responsibility and speak for themselves. The patterns of the liturgy should establish a shape and flow of the service that will become familiar to the participants.

The liturgy of the service orders and facilitates the encounter and conversation between the people and God. It is not by definition a fixed shape or structure, but more the processes by which the service is shaped to enable the meeting with God.

When the structures have failed to serve their needs in meeting God, church members tend to say they are abandoning liturgy but in fact most are looking to *renew* what historically has been called liturgy; the means by which the church is corporately present before God. Liturgy has provided re-enactment in symbolic form of the foundational truths of the Christian faith, thus teaching and nurturing the people. It has provided easily accessible forms for all to participate in word and action and acknowledgement that the leader is the facilitator of the people's worship through the liturgy - by making a structure in which the people are essential participants. Repetitiveness resulted in familiarity that meant that all could identify the shape and flow of the service, not only the leader. All could actively participate in declaration of faith, in intercession, in praise and acclamation, in obedience,

in confession. The concerns of leaders of all age worship are similar.

A sound liturgical structure helps the encounter with God, recognising the importance of inclusive and participatory forms that serve God and his people together. We recognise the need for symbolic action in addition to words as a form for participation. Identifiable shape, flow, and drama in the service are needed, and people should participate as fully as possible in the variety of elements: prayer, praise, and confession. The forms should be simple enough for most or all to participate actively. A structure is needed that results in open leadership that is not dependent of the charisma of one person or persons but may be extended as others are gifted to lead the service. There will be repetition so that the people can feel comfortable and recognise the means of participation.

The meaning of foundational truths will shape the service. For example: the presentation of the word of God in a service is a reflection of and extension of the reality of Christ coming into the world. Because the Word came into the world, we have access to the Father—so we come with prayer, intercession and thanksgiving; we have a firm hope—so we can declare our faith through the creeds; we are redeemed and are forgiven—so we can with confidence confess our sins; we are called to be disciples in the church and world—so we again offer ourselves in the offertory and in going out into the world.

Preparation

The preparation of a worship service includes consideration of bringing ourselves and collecting ourselves together consciously before God; listening to and hearing God's word in Scripture; responding to God in obedience, praise and offering; having opportunity to change and be renewed, receiving grace for following through on the word we have heard; being sent out to minister in the world.

Traditional liturgies, used and developed over the centuries of the church's history have much to contribute. Not that we should be backward looking, but they are a starting point, as they richly embody the functions for which liturgy is necessary. They may be to a certain extent rewritten, as the ASB is a thorough revision of the Book of Common Prayer. This is not to deny previous prayer books, but to bring the best of liturgy into contemporary language, using the richness of the form as a vehicle for worship.

Structured into the liturgy are the various aspects of a worship service covered in previous chapters, shaped in a manner that makes sense of the corporate nature of the gathering.

The call to worship can be any statement that recognises us and brings focus:

> We have been scattered
> Now we are together;
>
> We are in the world
> We serve in the name of Christ;
>
> We are gathered in fellowship
> In the presence of God.

This an example of the way that the leader may use a set of responses in which the people actively acknowledge the purpose of their gathering.

Setting aside of concerns and distracting thoughts happens in silence or in a simple corporate prayer, again an act of participation.

In confession together, the people acknowledge the continuing need for the redemptive work of God in the world and in them.

The service moves on to hearing God in the Scriptures and in reflection on its meaning, either through group reflection, drama or through preaching or teaching.

There is the means of responding to the word, for the people to say to God that they have heard the word and now intend to take action. The Creed helps make that declaration.

In the Peace, Christians offer to one another the *Shalom* greeting. This, in consideration of its Jewish origin, is a means of openly acknowledging that the life we have in Christ is a shared life in which we are connected to one another and we are committed to one another. In the peace, we offer wholeness to one another and offer to be one another's servants.

The thanksgiving of the people of Israel as they looked back over the Red Sea at the land from which they were delivered, was commemorated year by year. So in the passing seasons, liturgies acknowledge the key points of our faith and history, re-enacting and renewing our thanksgiving for those acts of God.

Intercession brings together the daily lives of the people and their calling to carry the gospel into the world. Many liturgical forms allow space for the congregation to voice these concerns in their own words, while the overall structure causes the church regularly to consider the work of the Church in the world in a broad way, causing them to think of concerns that may not have been newsworthy or closely tied to their own sphere of work and home life.

For there to be change in people's lives, for them to become more fully the people of God, they need grace from God. The church has many traditional ways to communicate grace, in the Eucharist, in Baptism, in the laying on of hands, in blessing one another in the Grace. In different circumstances and on various occasions these are built into the liturgy.

The end of a service includes prayers and blessings which finish the corporate time of praise and send the members out to fulfil the other necessary aspect of true worship, that is service in a multitude of ways, to be the church dispersed among the local community like yeast in the bread.

Leading Worship

Those who lead should recognise to whom they are speaking and state the words clearly and with intent—but not preaching or pressurising.

Using a simple phrase from the service, consider its content afresh, however familiar the words are to you:

"The Lord is here"—*the leader is telling what she knows*
"His Spirit is with us"—*the people respond in kind with what they know*

"The Lord is risen"—*re-enacts drama and speaks truth for today*

"He is risen indeed, Alleluia"—*the people state the truth that they too experience.*

In morning prayer such an introduction happens, then having stated their intent, the people approach God:

"Lord, open thou our lips
And our mouth shall proclaim your praise"

However familiar the service it is worth looking back over the words, for the weight of their meaning is profound. It is possible to consider the sentence "Glory to the Father, and to the Son, and the Holy Spirit: as it was in the beginning, is now, and shall be for ever. Amen," as a throwaway phrase at certain points in the service. Having looked anew at the meaning of the words, there is enormous and profound realisation of God in those few words and the simplest all-encompassing statement of praise. It was in reflection on those words that the reading 'Glory' on page 58 was written.

Sections of the service where the leader makes a statement and the people respond are often rooted in long tradition that has survived centuries of use. For at least 1600 years, the Orthodox churches have used the same Easter acclamation, quoted above, in their re-enactment of the Resurrection narrative when the priest leads the people into an exciting celebration of joy.

Areas of Question and Concern

People come to worship with a variety of feelings, a wide range of normal human emotions: excitement, depression, despair, anger, frustration, joy. The liturgy can offer a vehicle for those gathered to offer themselves to God with all their feelings:

"Lift up your hearts"
"We lift them to the Lord"

So we come with all our humanity, our strengths and weaknesses and are enabled to offer those to God. Such feelings are acceptable as an offering to God: remember that Jesus felt forsaken and gave that feeling to God in his cry on the Cross.

Contemporary individualism often demands personal satisfaction, appeasement of despair, demanding a sense or feeling of joy and excitement. These feelings may happen in worship but not necessarily. Nor are worship leaders there just to make the people feel good; they are there to help the people in worshipping God. We must expect worship to feel ordinary at least some of the time, hard work at others. A corporate presence in the world means we will suffer with Christ and it may not always feel good or satisfying! Worship is the work of the people, and a liturgy can help those present to be faithful in offering praise inclusive of a whole range of feelings. For example, together we confess our sin. I may feel pretty good about today, and feel right with God. But each week I spend the same as my neighbours (Christian and non-Christian) on food and goods. This may be no personal sin about which I feel guilty, but together with the rest of humanity, we in the Western nations are oppressive and destructive, having too much food while others in the world go without. The liturgy reminds us that feelings do not define the whole truth.

Spontaneity has its place in worship, but if over used, limits active participation, as it is unpredictable, and it is easier for a congregation to join in the expected and somewhat predictable. Similarly always to lead "spontaneously" results in limiting leadership to certain kinds of personality and the service will tend to belong to the leader.

An established liturgy is foundational to a faithful church as well as faithful members. In the history of the Orthodox Church, liturgy has been the means of its survival through persecution and adversity. If the church is dependent on inspired leadership, whose charisma holds it together, the leader can be removed and the church dies away. But if the liturgy and service are that of a whole people who simply need a leader to speak the introductions, they cannot be removed, shaken perhaps but not moved.

At the same time, there should be openness in the liturgy for spontaneity, for change and intervention of the Spirit, which could not be predicted or planned.

Developing a liturgy for all age worship

When a whole church gathers, including children and dependent people, not just the discipled more mature members, the encounter with God need be no less profound. A number of factors should be taken into account:

1. Include more active involvement, action as well as words.

2. Use simpler forms with less wordy responses.

3. Use visual forms, including symbolic actions such as lifting the bread during the consecration. Allow new

symbolic actions to develop; look to other churches and denominations for examples from the broad heritage that is ours.

4. Concentration spans are limited, so use briefer sections and shorter silences.

5. Encourage understanding of the service in the more mature members so they know how to help dependent members participate.

6. Have more tolerance in the structure; be able to bring the service back on course if something unexpected happens, as it will with children present. Be tolerant of reactions and responses. Adults have inward response, children outward ones. Check out what resulted in the response if the particular response is not helpful to the service.

7. Adults can be perfectionists and purists, so keep in mind the fact that the liturgy is a means to an end not an end in itself (consider this too for music and other elements). So if the liturgy is less than perfect in performance it may still have been an effective means.

8. Have an organic approach to liturgy, as a living form. Reflect on the service and adapt the ways and means:

   a. Does this facilitate worship?
   b. Why not?
   c. How could we improve?

Experiment with change, reflect and improve.

9. Provide all the congregation with books, even if they can't yet read. Help everyone find his or her place in the books, by a notice board, occasional announcement and by those nearby helping each other.

10. Do not use watered down versions of the liturgy; they tend to be patronising. Explain elements such as spontaneous worship so everyone may follow. Children are very attentive if they realise what they are listening for.

11. Children as well as adults appreciate a smooth-flowing service.

Looking at liturgy

Ritual and repetition are essential elements of good liturgy. Liturgy that includes all the congregation should use familiar words and phrases to say things that are familiar and accepted. The patterns of action with which the service develops should also be very familiar. At one time when I was running a playgroup, a three-year-old boy led his friends in playing church. He repeated the words and actions of the service he was part of each week—a sign of his absorption of the repetition and assimilation of what was happening.

Worship leaders may feel that the liturgy commonly used in their church is not all that they would desire. It may be possible to revise a liturgy to make it more appropriate for the congregation, but writing a new one is not likely in most circumstances to be highly successful, no more successful than the abandoned one. The patterns of traditional liturgies have stood the test of time and have evolved with people. The kind of revision used in developing the Anglican **Alternative Service Book** or even the change from Latin in the Roman Catholic Church are examples of revision that work. The value of the form is acknowledged and it is retained, but the language is updated to have more relevance. If you update the language of a liturgy, make sure that the new language is as rich in content as the original, that it flows well for spoken responses, has strong theological content. If you look at alternative services for all age worship consider them carefully as worship leaders. Would this liturgy assist the worship of all ages. Would you enjoy praising God with these words? If not, continue looking!

The language ought not to be class-bound, but be universal in its usage. The content must not be hidden in the language of a minority and not limited in scope to the concern or interests of a few. Hence, the liturgy should never be a children's liturgy or a theologian's liturgy, unless those are the only people present. The liturgy should reflect the fullness of traditional liturgies, both in the scope of the service in the aspects included and in the quality or richness of the language.

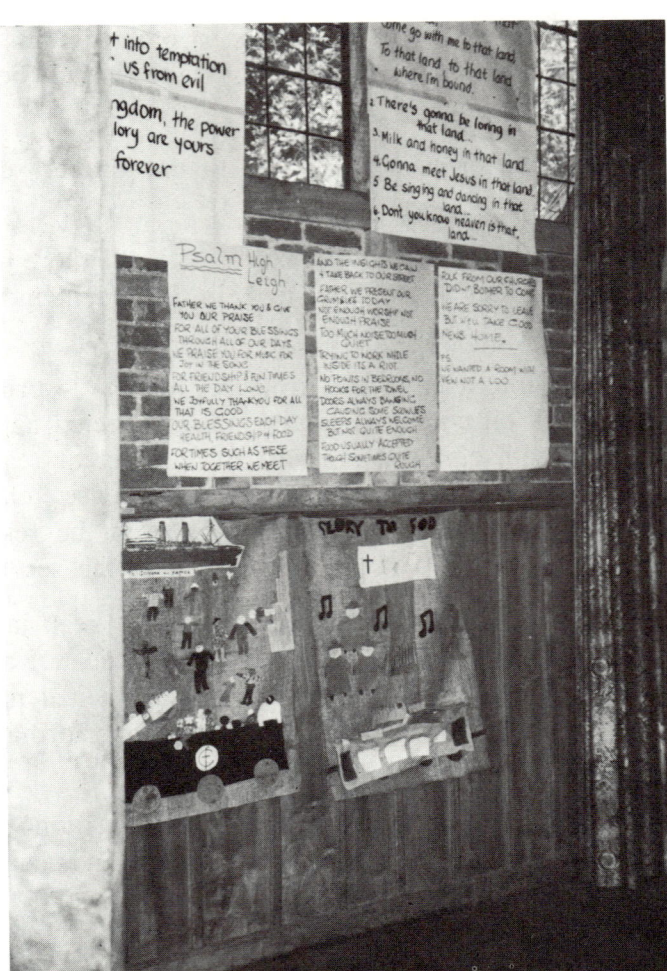

CHAPTER THIRTEEN: Atmosphere and Surroundings

A worship service is a significant event quite unlike the rest of our daily lives. Coming together as a congregation to worship involves touching on dimensions of experience that are uncommon; the people are gathered in a way that is peculiar to this time and purpose. The time is set aside as an offering to God, a time that is not assessed by the normal terms of daily existence and patterns. The definition of this time comes from the people's wish to worship and meet with God. Additionally the place of worship is of immense significance to the event; reverence and other qualities of worship grow out of all three, the people, the time, and the place. A sense of occasion is created through all three elements: the people in their expectation and offering of themselves; the time in being set aside as a kind of Sabbath that belongs to and is focussed on God; and the place, which is constructed, maintained and decorated to evoke an appropriate atmosphere for corporate worship.

A church building is a traditional place of worship. For the Jews from the time of Solomon, the temple was the centre for worship, as it was for Jesus and the apostles of the Early Church. Creation is an ideal arena for worship, with all creation is waiting for the fullness of time when it too will experience a redemption. However, we usually take ourselves inside a building, initially perhaps to escape the weather, but we have developed this context to make real a sense that we are entering a special time and place that is focussed on the mysteries and majesty of God. Cathedral and church builders through many ages have attempted to reflect the 'otherness' of God in the buildings they have designed and crafted, to reflect the majesty and the omnipotence of God and the awe and reverence of the human response. Church buildings have been filled with the signs of the Christian faith, not as mere memorials, but as living signs that affect our way of thinking and our way of interpreting everyday life. The surroundings and atmosphere in which we set worship are a major part of the creation of a worship service.

Worship is at least enhanced by the place in which it happens. On occasions when people arrive with their minds full of the confusion and anxieties of their own personal and family lives, simply walking into the atmosphere of the church can help them relax and be still in the presence of God. The liturgy can then offer them a vehicle for their praise.

Every building has shape and style related to its function, and those that are used for gatherings of people reflect the atmosphere that is desired for the gathering. A community hall is often a relatively bare open rectangular affair that lends itself as readily to the presentation of a pantomime, or a barn dance; a wedding reception, a bingo session, a political meeting, or a jumble sale. Because of its regular use for these functions, those who enter that hall associate their surroundings with those social occasions. A pub has its setting and layout designed around many small groups, clustered around small tables, with an atmosphere of intimacy.

In a parallel way, church buildings have established shapes that relates to their function in the lives of the local community. The building can enhance and serve the corporate gathering and simultaneously carries a sense of the mystery of God. The focus to which the eyes of the people are drawn suggests God. Hence there is the tradition of placing Christian signs and symbols at focal points. Worship in the round may suggest to the congregation that this is a corporate gathering before God, with the circle drawing attention also to the Eucharistic table or to the Bible—focussing on the Word present among the people.

Such aspects are vital to worship and worship planning. It is extremely difficult to establish all age worship in a lounge. Younger people associate the place with noisy play and the adults sit back and relax with the result that the congregation is slow in response to opportunities to participate actively and slow to sing and offer themselves wholeheartedly. At least for the duration of the service, the room should not feel or look like a lounge where people concentrate on themselves and each other, where they sit back and are entertained, or chatter to one another. Worship is helped considerably by additions that enhance worship, such as a table with cross and candle as the focus. Other additions could include banners and visual symbols that suggest this room at this time is dedicated to worshipping God.

Many churches are in the process of taking out their pews to replace them with chairs. This may be necessary for the creation of a sense of being God's people together—chairs set in the round can aid that understanding. Space may be needed for participatory expressions of worship, for dance and drama. But care must be taken in changing from pews to chairs that the layout is still evocative of worship, intensifying not distracting. Most members of the church will like to see a familiar layout when they enter the building on most Sundays, but for festivals will enjoy finding that the setting is unusual—to help create a sense of excitement a special occasion. In moving the seating to face a different direction, remember to create a new visual focus as well. It is not very helpful for the congregation to find themselves turned away from a chancel that is rich in symbols and signs, to face a blank side wall, marked only by several memorial brasses.

If your church is large but your congregation small, find ways to arrange the seating that bring the people closer together physically. Try blocking off or removing the back rows of seats, building in a dividing screen that blocks off half the room, or even bringing the Communion table nearer to the people, on the chancel steps or into what was the aisle. People who worship in a thinly spread scattered way, will think of God's people being a thinly scattered remnant!

Many older church buildings were designed in the days of candlelight and lamps. The introduction of bright white light, especially strip lighting, creates a clinical cold atmosphere as the light reflects off hard stone walls. If you have opportunity to consider the installation of lighting, experiment to find what will enhance the warmth of fellowship. Use yellower lighting that does not glare and separate people. Use indirect lighting where possible - spotlights on the focal points in the building also throw light back onto the people, while lights that hang lower give a greater sense of intimacy. For special occasions such as Advent and Christmas, when light is major element of the theme, use special lighting effects such as candles. The whiteness of paintwork and lighting can be an asset when it is used as a background to visually warming additions such as banners and colourful vestments.

It is hard to worship in a cold building while wearing your outdoor coat. We may work to establish a worshipping service but cold tends to separate and distance people; they rush away home as soon as possible to get warm. Make sure the heating is set high enough for people to want to take off their outdoor coats.

Carpeting can help worship! Carpets absorb sound, and in a building that is large and echoing, carpet reduces extraneous noise, absorbing the sound of a child's noisy toy. When the aisle and chancel are carpeted the church building may feel more welcoming and less austere and forbidding. Then too, the carpet adds to the colour and warmth of the atmosphere.

Vestments, robes, candles, and processions all add to the sense of occasion, that this is a special and different time. Signs such as vestments, with all their splendid colours, create a rich environment for assimilating the meaning and mystery of the Christian faith.

People and atmosphere

When people, both adults and children, arrive at church, the greeting of the stewards at the door is an important gift to worship. Stewards can receive people in a friendly, open and helpful manner. They should greet people with respect and concern, helping them to prepare for worship. They may help some to a seat, and by their manner stewards may help the noisy be a little quieter and assure everyone they are welcome in God's presence. It is helpful if the stewards can look out for more shy people and greet them, and if they can learn the names of children as well as adults.

Consider in advance where each person involved in leading the service is to be seated, both during the time of their contribution and before it. Each must have easy access to a seat rather than be struggling along a row when the reading or prayer should have started. Look for smooth flow. Find a position for the music group from which they can be seen and lead without being in the way as people go forward for Communion.

Your church may need amplification for some of those present. Make sure that this is properly prepared and is not intrusive visually or aurally. The system should be used to add just a little to the sound but not be strident. Can your system be developed to include a loop for the deaf members also? Teach readers to speak out clearly regardless of whether there is a microphone helping the sound; no one should whisper or mumble the reading.

In preparing the service setting, do not expect children to do what adults don't. If adults are rushing round before the service begins, so will the children: the service will begin in a flurry of noise, and the call to worship will be acknowledged only with difficulty. If the service is to be solemn or reverent, then the preparation must also be. Those leading a service should be totally prepared and ready by the time the congregation begins to arrive, some minutes before the service. The leaders could even be seated in their places ready. The leaders can pray together, beginning to focus consciously on God before they begin to lead others and this is best achieved in quietness and calm. If someone realises at the last minute that something has been overlooked, this should be attended to quietly and without hurry or anxiety.

When newcomers are present for worship, it is the responsibility of stewards and those around them to help them find their way through the service as necessary. Make sure they have all the books to hand and that someone nearby is alert to help them find the place in the books as needed. Children often need help, especially if they have come unattended by an adult. In this case as with newcomers, other members of the congregation should expect to move to sit next to them in order to help them follow through the liturgy.

Banner making

There are useful books on banner making in most Christian bookshops and a section of the *Workshop* on page 129 includes banner making.

When preparing a banner background, consider the shape of the space in which you intend to hang the banner. Make sure the banner shape is compatible with the wall space and that the banner is big enough.

Consider the liturgical setting, the season and its colour, so the banner is in harmony with the vestments. Place the banner fabrics against the vestments to check that they blend with one another.

Simple designs communicate best—one idea is plenty on any banner. Signs and symbols are more effective than words on most occasions. If explanatory words seem necessary, then probably the banner idea is too complex for the situation.

When a group is working together on a banner, as in the Workshop, the theme may be simple, though the design may be fairly detailed.

CHAPTER FOURTEEN: Planning and Preparation

For most churches all age worship is a recurring event, often a monthly service plus the festivals of the church year. Those churches who have a weekly all age Parish Communion should in addition look at Chapter Sixteen and at the list of books in the appendix. The all age worship service is one in which it is becoming customary to include a variety of people in leadership and it is for all those involved that this chapter goes into detailed aspects of planning particular services as well as considering the necessity of longer term development.

The Planning Group

The leadership gifts that are called into action when all age worship is being developed and prepared come from all departments of church life. The following gifts may be expressed by several people but should be present to provide a balanced planning session that takes into account the breadth of the church's life.

There should be a liturgist, a person with a sense of the flow of the service and the pieces large and small that should be in place for worship to be developed. This person is aware of the Spirit, aware of the effect of disruption, aware of how music, words, and theme relate to one another in the leadership of worship. There should also be an awareness of the Church generally and its life of which the local church is a part; this is partly expressed in an understanding of the seasons of the Church year and of the shape and relevance of the lectionary.

The group, if a Eucharistic service is being prepared, must include the priest.

Pastoral oversight of the church should be represented, someone who brings a concern for the overall life and health of the church as a body, knowing its development, and whether themes of discipleship, repentance, hope or faith are relevant to its growth to maturity. There should also be understanding of the pastoral care of individuals, of any particular problems that individuals are struggling with. Though the particulars of these may not be disclosed to the group, this person, a counsellor usually, will be prepared to help those she counsels integrate the teaching and worship into their own lives.

Musicians should be represented, especially the person who selects music and teaches the choir. If a music group plays at the services, the leader ought also to be present.

If your church has a Sunday School or youth programme, these should be represented as, effectively, the teachers have pastoral care of the children and understand their nurture and education in the church.

Some churches may add to this drama and dance group leaders.

This may now sound like a very large group! However, you may find that one person represents several aspects, or you may have this large group meet occasionally for long-term planning and use a smaller subgroup for the detailed work. In a large and active church, the large group is appropriate and can learn to work together.

A planning group that represents many aspects of church life can bring together the variety of threads to be woven into the one service. But do not make the mistake of automatically making such a group into the leaders of the service; they may not be worship leaders! Some people have a charisma and understanding for leading worship services that is necessary even when a group shares leadership. One or two people must have charge of the service and develop a common understanding of their aims, be able to communicate easily, sort out differences of opinion and problems readily. The qualitites of the worship leaders are more fully covered in Chapter Two, page 13. The relationship of the planning group to those leaders is vital and must be built on mutual trust, and on recognition of one another's gifts. Decisions should come from mutual agreement that depends on the group being able to pray and hear God together.

No member should have the power of veto, but nor should the group override one person's concern. Those who counsel individuals in the church may ask for a time for prayer for healing during the course of the service. Others may see this to be difficult: those leading the service may worry about the time these prayers would take and that children might become restless; others may be concerned that this would distract from the theme of the service. The group could decide to handle this concern in several ways: an additional special healing service, a brief prayer during the administration of communion, or prayer in a side chapel, but they may not dismiss the concern as irrelevant. Similarly, if the children's leaders recognise that the children or their parents find aspects of the all age worship services difficult, the group should creatively discuss the problem.

Themes

The themes for all age worship services should begin in long-term planning. Themes should represent seasonal and festival themes from the church year. They should be seen as general to the whole Church of God, and specific to this particular church. The planning group should first discuss together the way in which a particular theme, such as Easter, fits into the history of the Church, how it reflects this particular season in creation, how various churches have celebrated Easter historically and in contemporary ways, and how this church has previously recognised and taught about Easter in services and in children's programmes. Out of this wealth of information and background material, the group may select a focus or central theme for the service, with other aspects adding colour and richness to the services within that season.

Such advance consideration allows for worship leaders, musicians, drama group leaders and others, to consider how that theme might be developed. The music leaders can go through the church's repertoire of hymns and songs selecting suitable material; they can look for new music for the congregation to learn or an anthem for the choir. Sunday School leaders or the drama and dance leaders could consider ideas for ways in which the theme could be developed in participatory ways. At a further meeting, when the specific details of each service are filled in, these resources may be dovetailed together, selecting from among the possibilities.

As the planning group becomes more experienced in working together some ideas and resources may be consolidated at the initial meeting, but this is not always possible if new members are going to be able to contribute constructively. Not everyone can think fast, especially when inexperienced, and would like time to reflect on the theme themselves. This will be especially true if church members write their own resource materials, drama or dance, as the ideas need time to germinate and be developed into something concrete.

Specific planning of services

The planning group should begin the specific planning for each particular service with time in hand for preparation and rehearsal as necessary. Last-minute planning works only if the service is to use the established repertoire of the congregation, and if all the teaching and leading is done by one person or at the most two, upon whom all the responsibility falls. Developing shared leadership and shared responsibility, and using the gifts of inexperienced lay leaders takes time.

The teaching theme is first put into words. The teaching or sermon should reflect the history and theology relevant to the theme, should be clearly biblically based. It should have contemporary relevance to society and yet be localised and human in its appeal. The presentation and communication should be clear, informative, encouraging and challenging. The speaker should be able to make the theme relevant to all ages and be brief. Brevity is not the same as oversimplifying, but the sermon should have a key point that is the theme of the service, and the rest of the words set this in context and show how this is relevant to all the people present.

If it is not relevant to all those present, then look again at how the general theme was narrowed down, and revise your plans.

Once the theme has been made specific, share among the group ideas for music, drama and dance and other participatory aspects. There may be many ideas, but all will not be used. The resultant service plan should be coherent, uncluttered, and straight-forward and those who are to be at the front leading the service must be happy that the chosen elements fit and flow smoothly out of each other without distracting from the purpose of praising God. Not every service will have a dramatic presentation or dance. Not every service will have a new song or hymn.

Create the right atmosphere for people to walk into before the service even starts, create a sense of the occasion. Consider the non-verbal aspects of the service and the setting. Would banners be a helpful addition? What movement should there be to enhance the theme? What practical preparations are necessary, from talking with stewards and readers to printing service sheets?

When a service is being prepared, consider the overall visual effect and look for new ideas to add to the setting. It is possible to use a large cross for Good Friday, use darkness and candles in Advent, create sombre gloom in Lent, fill the church with brightness on festivals.

Once the overall plan for the service has been mapped out, consider the liturgy in detail and how all these elements fit together and how the flow will be maintained. If a special item is being added, can this be covered with

101

a prior announcement, by the service sheet, or should there be a brief sentence said at the time. If your plans affect the normal order of the liturgy, consider carefully whether this is necessary, as people may easily become confused and therefore distracted from worship.

Just prior to the service, all those with leadership roles should meet and run through the outline, so all are conscious of the elements and can then pray together.

Everyone whose participation is key to the flow of the service should have a written out schedule of the service to avoid unnecessary breaks or confusion. At services where there is a lot of movement, such as at a festival service, those who share leadership should be aware at all times who is in charge of the event. Musicians may have charge of a time of spontaneous worship—not the priest. In this case it is important for there to be a clear changeover from one to the other. When the musicians hand the responsibility back to the priest for the closing prayers, to avoid confusion there can be a tiny but clear signal such as a nod from the music group leader.

Planning groups should meet again after the service to reflect on the service, how it went and how snags might be dealt with in future. We all learn from mistakes.

CHAPTER FIFTEEN: Discipline

The basis for any discipline of children in church is primarily focussed on their full membership and participation; it is not based on keeping children quiet, seen but not heard, while everyone else gets on with worship. Discipline in a worship service is based on the understanding that all discipline is working towards self-discipline and in worship this involves offering every opportunity and encouragement for all those present to participate fully. Children are being helped to join in the act of worship along with the older members. All *correction* of the child is on this foundation, just as correction of a child at a family meal table is focussed on helping the child feed herself and join the family fellowship. Try the following experiment with a group of adult friends: provide each person with a piece of string one yard long. With the string each person ties her feet together, then instruct everyone to sit on their hands. Now tell everyone to close their mouths until you give them permission to open them again. Now begin talking about an issue they know nothing about, such as something technical to do with your work or your filing system. The point is soon apparent to all.[1]

A person's concentration span is approximately one minute for each year of age, up to a maximum of twelve minutes. The average adult finds after a while that his attention has wandered and brings himself back to a consciousness of what is happening around him and a child is the same, though her concentration span is shorter and adults may help bring her attention back. It is possible to concentrate for longer if the activity involved is more than listening, is participatory, or has a strong visual or dramatic element to it.

There are churches who have a predominance of young families with under-five-year-olds and find the inclusion of so many children difficult. Churches on the other hand who have been multi-generational for longer have a much easier time with all age worship. For the former churches it may seem for a while that they are overwhelmed by the presence of so many young members, and adults who are accustomed to worship and focus on God in a quieter atmosphere find the sounds of children and the changes to acknowledge their presence extremely uncomfortable. It may at first seem impossible really to worship. Yet there are processes which a congregation, leaders and parents, may adopt to assist in bringing all ages together in worship.

There are aspects to discipline that concern the worship leaders; others concern the parents who bring children; still others concern single adults and married couples without children. All these people are part of making the ethos in which all age worship can be a full expression of worship by the congregation together.

0—2 year-olds

The worship service is not child-centred but God-centred, and the parent is functioning as a worship leader to the child he has in his arms. The focus of worship is on God, so the focus of the adult carrying a baby or toddler is on God at the same time as he is aware of the ways he can help his child join in. That is not possible continuously because of the needs of the child, but the rest of the congregation and the leaders help by providing a strong worship structure and form on which the adult and the child can depend.

The parent sits where the child has the best view possible, seeing the movement, the candles, the readers, the visual signs of worship. It is not easy to join in worship when the child is dependent on the non-verbal if all that he can see is the back of a row of heads.

The parent provides as far as possible for both the child and himself to join in all the participatory aspects of the service. Have a service book, preferably one with pictures. Have appropriate bible story picture books during the presentation of the word. Use an illustrated children's Bible. Of course there are times when aspects of the service are not drawing the child's attention, so have a few quiet toys available, avoiding those that would distract other children with the noise they make. Pool ideas with other parents to find toys that are ideal.

Talking between parent and toddler will happen frequently in questions and explanations. By example and by instruction teach the child to whisper; that's not as hard as it may at first sound and can begin with the child of 15 to 18 months.

A small child must move; she cannot sit still for ages, so use every possible movement with her. The parent should sit, stand, and kneel with the child as everyone else does. As soon as she can walk, hold her hand and let her walk up to the Communion rail at the Eucharist service. Children do move and listen at the same time; a child who is swinging his feet and playing quietly may be fully aware of the words he is hearing. The activity of a small child is something that the congregation itself may need to learn to accommodate, knowing that parents and other adults are helping the children join in as much as possible. However, don't let toddlers run riot. A child who is filling her time with busy self-centred activity and noise will distract herself and others from the intended focus of worship.

A baby may cry because he is tired, or teething, or has colic. Take him to the back of the church and stand rocking him or take him outside for a few minutes till he is less distressed. A baby may be distressed frequently and parents often lose time at worship services. Other adults who are close to the family may take a turn holding the baby or walking with him so parents can participate more fully.

An older toddler may need correction during the service, or is having a tantrum or making unreasonable demands: the parent can take him outside, telling him that they will return to the service as soon as he is quiet and ready to join in with everyone else.

It is very helpful to families, parents and children if there are other adults who are well known to the children. In this case it is very easy for those other adults to share the tasks of helping a child during a service, holding him, or taking him outside for a few minutes.

When a family has several small children, family friends can make a regular point either of inviting one of the children to sit with them, or of themselves sitting with the family to help children to take part in the service.

3—6 year-olds

Every child in this age group should have books to follow during the service, both song books and prayer books, preferably with pictures. Children of this age group very much want to take part with everyone else, so will most often copy the behaviour of older children around them. Leaders and parents and older children in the church can talk together about what they are wanting during the service; as older children find they are able to participate more fully the younger ones follow, by imitation. The older children sympathise and help with younger ones. During the wedding I mentioned previously, at which the priest invited the children up to stand with him while the couple made their vows and exchanged rings, the children clustered around the altar watching intently. I saw that six-year-old Megan had a firm grasp on the hand of her small sister and was explaining to her in whispers what was happening.

The parent accompanying the preschool child can help him join in as fully as possible in the way that older children and adults are participating. When the child has a contribution for the prayer time, the parent may voice it for him. Help him see who is praying when there are contributions from the congregation. The physical actions are easier to imitate than the verbal responses but many children in this age group also have song words that they know by heart and can sense when to say 'amen' with everyone else.

Sit in the front seats so the child can see all that happens, especially for services that are rich in movement, such as the Communion service. Make sure that the stewards know the child's name and help him say 'Hello' to them, collecting a book like others of all ages. Encourage the child to sing when others sing, even when he doesn't know the words, to kneel when others kneel to pray, to be silent when others are silent.

Seven—plus

Children of this age group, from top infants and the middle school, are fully active and involved in every aspect of the service. They give and take along with the rest of the congregation. They read, act, operate puppets, serve, act as stewards, dance, and care for others in every way—if given the opportunity.

If you use the workshop (Chapter Eighteen) to prepare services, children of this age will be very creative and help adults in offering worship, using ways that are a common expression for all ages. When given such opportunity children will write songs, drama and modern parables.

Don't underestimate children, as they have great potential, given a chance, to work alongside others of their own age and of all ages in the church.

Leaders

The service where there are lots of children in the youngest age groups need not be chaotic. Start with a clear, well-defined and concise structure, with timings written in for each part of the liturgy. Learn not to over-run on timings, so the service is crisp without being hurried. When the services have an established flow, movement, and development then it may be possible, if this is justified by the needs of the whole congregation, to make aspects of the service longer. A baptism may lengthen the morning Communion service, but if the rest of the service flows, the extra time will work perfectly well for the youngest members. But if the service overruns because there was 'dead time' when presentation was sluggish, then children quickly lose concentration because there is nothing for them to focus on. Don't hurry the service or think it has to be snappy or fast—but it must not be sloppy. If the service regularly overruns look again at the way it is led. Maybe there are too many leaders with too many change-overs, or some sections are always too long. Find a creative way to deal with these issues as a leadership group.

Parents as partners

Parents and leaders have a vital partnership in all age worship. The leaders can develop a viable form for the congregation in which all may be included, and the parents and other adults can help the children take this opportunity. Parents and worship leaders should talk together about what is helpful and what is not for each of their roles in the service, how they help or hinder one another. Parents who are not leaders of the service may have very helpful ideas as a result of their own conversations with children.

New Families

New families come into church with their children. If they are not church-going families simply transferring their membership, there may be helpful action that regular church-goers can offer.

One inner city church had many young families join them from the neighbourhood, with no previous experience of church. The mid-week Mother and Toddler Group resulted in good friendships between the new and established parents who were then able to sit together. It was easier for the new parents to see that help with their children was readily available—and the help was not a hidden criticism!

In other churches, where many new families arrive with no expectation of controlling the children's behaviour (or ability to), the congregation have learned to struggle on with the worship against this background of disorder. Families who continue to come gradually adopt the approach of longer-established families, but it is hard on the church in the meantime. Find a balance between softening the extraneous noise by having carpeted floor and turning up the amplification just a little.

Notes:

1. Idea from Dave Holmes, Rock Rapids, US.

CHAPTER SIXTEEN: All Age Worship and the Eucharist

Eucharist is celebrated on a pattern instituted by Christ; we celebrate it as a sign of our obedience till he comes again, as a sign of our redemption into being God's own people, as a sign that we are with Christ, and he with us, in his sacrifice, his ministry, and in his coming in glory. It is a symbolic action in that we have a real sharing among us of one loaf and the reality that Christ is present in the one body of our life and worship.

There is a continuing debate about the rightness, or not, of children receiving the sacrament, but this chapter will not present the various threads and questions, theological and doctrinal, that a full debate would represent. However, the case for children's full participation in the Eucharist will be outlined as a preliminary to suggestions, based on experience, for children receiving the sacrament.

The church that wishes to develop a life and worship that is fully inclusive of children, and especially those for whom the Parish Communion is the key service of the week, will find this chapter to be of particular interest and help.

Why include children at the Lord's Table?

Eugene Brand, in the Grove Liturgical Study no. 44, wrote "the proper answer to the question of the communion of children is crucial to their own spiritual formation as individuals, their understanding of the faithful participation in the Church's worship, and their grasp of the corporate character of the Church. But that is only the beginning. It is also crucial to the development of a full and natural spirituality in the families of the Church and to the success of the catechetical efforts of the parents. And finally it is crucial to the health of the local community, keeping it liturgically and spiritually flexible and preserving it from an arid intellectualism. Acting on the fact that baptized children are full members of the community could bring alive many a dull and dreary congregation!"[1]

The full participation of babies and children in the Eucharist has first to be seen in the light of the theology and history of the Church.[2]

The first examples of this in the Early Church in the Acts of the Apostles, are not very clear on the participation of children, though the earliest writings do show that to separate Baptism from the Eucharist was inconceivable. Baptism was the sacrament of initiation into the Church, and all who entered received the Sacrament. In 246 AD, Cyprian wrote in more detail about the practice of the church and participation in the Christian community. He declared that "Infants are as capable of baptism as are adults and share equally in the divine gift given in baptism. Having thus been baptized in the Spirit the newborn drink thereon from the Lord's cup, and are thus both 'baptized and sanctified'." It is baptism and eucharist which together establish and maintain membership of the Christian community. "Baptism and Eucharist are inseparable and for Cyprian it is the Eucharist that creates the Christian community. To abandon the Eucharist is to abandon the community and to abandon either is to abandon Christ."[3]

As history unfolded over the next two centuries, the case developed, with Augustine seeing children as ideal recipients of the Eucharist, those who are images of the helplessness of the human being before his parents. The Orthodox churches have changed their practice very little since those days. However the Western churches have gone through many changes and stages in their concept of children and the Eucharist. In the twelfth century the practice was largely dropped, as Baptism was separated from the Eucharist and the chalice was separated from the laity. Several reforming movements in the middle ages reintroduced sharing the sacraments with children but not without opposition.

The position of the reformers was summarised by one of them, Matthias, who was concerned for "...the poor and disenfranchised ...who in their simplicity might well not be able to 'discern the body' in any articulate manner. ... To suggest any grounds for qualification other than baptism is unthinkable. The child thus becomes the image of the perfect communicant."[4]

The concern in subsequent centuries that the body be properly discerned meant the practice of infant Communion was never again fully established. In later centuries, those who were to be admitted to the Lord's Table had to be seen to be living a godly life and to answer questions put to them by their minister. The situation has changed very little, as those preparing for confirmation, the rite of entry to communion, have been taught basic truths of the faith as the means of entry into the Eucharist and adult membership of the church.

But the position is being questioned and practice is changing in various parts of the Anglican communion. Why? It may seem blatantly obvious that no one can really *understand* the sacraments, certainly not in any simple examination set for adolescent young people. The key reason for change is almost undoubtedly in the nature of the community of faith in contemporary society. A secular or post-Christian society is no longer supportive, and is often cynical and antagonistic, so the Church is finding it necessary to reassert its identity as a Christian community that is in contrast to the society around it: a problem not faced since the establishment of the Church. Into this realisation and reassessment comes the understanding that for the Early Church the sacraments were inseparable and together were the initiation into the community and that babies and children were seen as ideally those who would receive. Most recently it has been affirmed that there is not one kind of baptism for adults and another for children, the former only leading to the Eucharist; there is only one Baptism.

Patterns of Worship

The inclusion of children at the heart of the Eucharistic worship raises questions for the whole service, not just the practices of administration. There are several common patterns of Parish Communion in which children are part-time participants. On one pattern they are present for the opening song and call to worship then they depart for separate lessons during the presentation of the word and the intercessions, returning for the Peace. On another pattern, which gives the children more time for a Sunday School lesson they first join the congregation at the Peace or Offertory song. Both patterns are inadequate as children are fully members of the Christian community by Baptism and the Eucharist is an essential element in their belonging and nurture in the body of the Church.

The service is a whole and it is shaped as a drama with a flow and development that points always to the Word, in a first climax which is the reading and preaching and a second greater highpoint in the Word incarnate in the sacraments. To bring in the children half-way through the drama is to bring them into a story that is half told. If the church chooses to maintain a style of worship that is planned around the worship offering of just the adults maybe it is a mercy to the children that they come in half way through. But this misses the essential consequences of seeing Baptism and Eucharist as the sacraments of the people of God and the foundation of all age worship. If all are equal in the grace of baptism and the participation in the Lord's Supper, then the rest of the service that contextualises those in offering worship to God should also be primarily a service for all the baptised without discrimination. The explanation of how this may happen is to summarise and contextualise the other chapters of this book.

The Eucharist as set out in the common and traditional liturgies, the **Alternative Service Book**, and others such as the **American Book of Common Prayer**, are full of symbolism and drama. It is possible for the development of the service to be expressed in words alone, with no movement from the people and very little from the priest and other leaders. However, when looking at the service as an offering of worship from all ages, the potential for movement and symbolic action should be exploited to its fullest. For some members of the congregation, the verbal has little meaning, but the active, visual and participatory presentation in worship can be inclusive and nurturing.

Learning to present mime is perhaps a good parallel using the potential for movement fully. Take whatever movement is already there and make it a little bigger and clearer, more visual. When beginning the service, use the processional fully: light candles, build the sense of occasion in the movement and visual actions. Sing as many parts of the service as may be set to music in a form that is rich but congregational. The readings may be complex; if there is a story, perhaps a drama could retell it; readers come among the people for the gospel, bringing the candles and the congregation may stand. Add a song before or after the gospel reading.

In most Parish Communion services, the full service results in there being a brief sermon even when the children are not present! So continue to keep the sermon brief and to the point. Use your best and most coherent preachers for all age worship. Illustrate the talk with drama, pictures, banners, action, symbolism as far as possible; all the congregation will remember it longer, not just the children. But remember the importance of the Word and do not detract from its fullness by being patronising, simplistic or unchallenging. When leading intercessions that present the concerns of the people, do so with the participation of as many members as possible. Have an active exchange of the Peace, greeting one another with a handshake or a friendly hug. We are all ministers of the grace of God and in the Peace we give peace to one another, old and young.

The offertory in its movement and symbolic action can include the bringing forward of the bread and wine as well as the money offerings. Hold up each of them as the appropriate words are spoken. Have all ages take part in collecting the offering and carrying it forward. The Thanksgiving can seem a long and hard prayer even for adults. Use a series of participatory teachings to contextualise the content and the poetry of these prayers. Then use all possible symbolic action, lifting up the elements so they are clearly visible; no liturgical action should be lost to the sight of the congregation. This is not to create a false ritualism but to communicate in action as well as words.

As the congregation come forward to receive the bread and wine, children almost without fail assimilate and adopt for themselves the attitude they see in the adults and if any reminder is given, it is quickly accepted. Kneel to receive the elements and teach children to lay one hand on top of other and to say 'Amen' as they receive. Each action reinforces the sense of occasion and significance of the event.

Children may bring elements of joy, delight, excitement and curiosity, visible on their faces at least, that is seldom present with adults alone. If adults in the congregation sit and daydream after receiving the elements or even exchange the occasional whisper to one another, the children will receive the message that it is time to relax but they will speak more loudly! Consider the focus of the whole congregation during the administration, as the congregation gradually go forward, then help everyone focus during this time. If this is a time of silent prayer teach adults and children to kneel and pray quietly. If this is a time of quiet adoration and worship then there can be congregational songs that quietly offer glory and thanks to God.

If there are recurrent problems with children at particular points in the service, ask yourselves if the leaders know what action or participation they are expecting of the congregation at that point (perhaps listening). Is the congregation aware of this appropriate response, and are the leaders helping the congregation to respond this way? If the congregation has been sitting listening for half an hour then the leaders are not helping them at this point. Look again at movement and participation overall.

Questions for Group Reflection

For churches who wish to discuss further the participation of children in the Eucharist, the following discussion questions may be of help.

1   In what practical ways can we give children a sense that they are participating members of the church?

2   What do we discern the body of Christ to be in our church?

3   What do we discern the Sacrament to be in our Eucharist? What do we see it representing?

4   Are children members of what we see the body of Christ to be?

5   What barriers stand between the church adopting a policy of baptism being the Sacrament of admission to the church and the Eucharist?

6   Given the reservations expressed in the above questions, would you as a group recommend that:

The church move towards children receiving the elements in the Eucharist, as a necessary corollary to their having been baptised?

If you consider favourably a move towards children participating fully in the Eucharist, what changes do you recommend to your current practices, in principle and in particular.

How can children learn, as appropriate to their age, what they are joining and receiving?

Teaching for All Ages

While the gathering together for all age worship is an essential ingredient of the life of local church, there is a continuing need for teaching appropriate to ages and development.

Both in the form of Sunday Schools and Children's Church, many of our young people are receiving excellent knowledge of the Christian faith. Many adults receive their teaching in the Sunday sermons or in mid-week Bible studies.

When members of a church gather only on Sunday mornings and children have an established pattern of going to Sunday School during the service, how can both these essential needs be met? There are several possible ways.

If the majority of the Sunday morning congregation also attend mid-week meetings for Bible study or for children's groups, then having everyone together on Sunday mornings may not create undue pressure on the teaching programme. The latter can be effectively covered as groups meet separately during the week.

If most of the congregation can only be present on Sunday mornings, and there are many reasons for this being the case, two courses of action may be considered. First it may be possible to follow the pattern of many British churches and have all age worship services once a month with, on the other Sundays, groups meeting separately for teaching and worship. Alternatively, the pattern adopted by many churches on the United States could best meet the needs of members. Sunday morning begins with Sunday School for all ages including adults, each going to their own groups. This is followed by a short break after which the whole congregation gathers for all age worship. There are many advantages to this latter scheme especially when it is difficult for a congregation to gather midweek.

Notes

1. "Nurturing Children in Communion" edited by Colin Buchanan, Grove Liturgical Booklet 44.

2. "Infant Communion—Then and Now" David Holeton, Grove Liturgical Booklet 27.

3. Ibid.

4. Ibid.

5. Consider the "King of Glory" musical setting for the Eucharist, published by Celebration and available through your local Christian bookshop or from Celebration, 58 High Street, Bletchingley, Surrey, RH1 4PA.

CHAPTER SEVENTEEN: Festivals

There are occasions in the Church year when all ages in the church gather to remember, to affirm and to celebrate the important events in the life of the Church. Some festivals are recollections of the Church's history—saints' days for example—others are key events for the local church—an induction, baptism or confirmation service. Still others are the services which reflect the Church's history and tradition—Easter and Pentecost are two such celebrations.

On any or all of these events, special preparation may be made for the service. Often people who are marginal to the church will be present. The regular congregation expect rich and festive offering of worship, with music, colour and liturgy reflecting the significance of the day. For such occasions all ages within the church will be ready to spend extra time in preparation: making banners and vestments, holding extra choir rehearsals, preparing in Sunday School, and rehearsing drama.

The scripts in this chapter are resources for festivals and other occasions when a more ambitious presentation is appropriate. It is anticipated that there would be several rehearsals and a relatively polished performance within a festive service.

THE CHRISTMAS SPACE TRAVELLERS

The scene involves the Space Travellers locating themselves in the balcony, or other location distant and higher than the main playing area.

In our church production, we had a shiny star on nylon thread, which led from the balcony down to front of the church so the Wise Men could follow it. The star was under the charge of the adult whose additional task was to keep an eye on the exuberant Space Travellers and prompt them if necessary.

Characters: Nick, Christopher, Jane, Esther, Ian, Darren, -- the Space Travellers.
> Alice, Katharine, Hannah -- the angels
> Andrew and others, shepherds
> Dawn and others, -- kings
> Mary, Joseph

Many other children had non-speaking parts as angels, shepherds and kings. Older children partnered the 3-5-year-olds so they arrived at the right place at the right time.

Costumes: Traditional for nativity characters. Any available metallic looking clothes for Space Travellers, for example: Wellington boots were covered with tin foil, motorbike helmets also covered in foil but worn only when they walk to the stage (or they can't hear).

The stage area is set with crib, and a baby doll is hidden behind Mary's chair. One angel passes the baby to Mary at the appropriate moment.

The crib is centre stage; the angels stand in a line behind the holy family; the shepherds enter and group stage left, some sitting; the kings enter stage right and kneel to offer gifts. The Space Travellers begin on the balcony and come to stand on the floor, below and in front of the stage, looking at the crib.

Have lights on the stage and over the balcony, so the Space Travellers are also clearly visible.

(**Mary** *and* **Joseph** *are onstage,* **Space Travellers** *enter on balcony*)

Nick: Here we are at last, landed on earth. Now we will look at some real earth people.

Christopher: It is a very strange place, isn't it? It's not at all like our planet.

Mark: Their systems are different. For a start there is air all around them and they breathe it in and out. And they have soft skin and hair.

Jane: God had quite a good idea when he made them, didn't he?

Christopher: I heard on the galactic information channel that they have had problems. The first ones God made got into trouble, they sinned. It's been getting worse ever since.

Mark: I heard that God nearly cancelled them all out with a flood. He only saved Noah.

Jane: It is a pity they are such a bad lot.

Esther: But God doesn't just give up, you wait and see. I bet he does something.

Ian: There is something going on over there. Look! It's a bright light. Is it more space travellers?

(**Angels** *enter and walk onto stage*)

Darren: (*to angels*) Hello, you people over there. What is happening?

Alice: We are angels on the way to Bethlehem.

Katharine: God has sent his son into the world. We have come to worship him.

Hannah: We are going to the stable to see the baby.

(*All angels on stage*)

Jane: There's another crowd over there. What are they doing, getting up in the middle of the night?

(**Shepherds** *enter*)

Mark: (*to* **Shepherds**) Ahoy, earth people. What is happening tonight? Where are you going?

Andrew: Those angels told us there's a king being born in a cowshed in Bethlehem. We are going to see. We have left our sheep on the hillside.

Nick: A king in a cowshed! Goodness, that is strange!

Christopher: What is a king? And why is it strange for him to be born in a cowshed?

Nick: A king is someone in charge, like an emperor on our planet. Usually they are born in huge, rich palaces and castles. It is not likely that one would be born in a cowshed.

Jane: This is a good time to come here. We can see what happens next.

(*Star moves slowly across the sky*)

Esther: Look! Over there!

Ian: Is it a shooting star?

(*Enter* **Kings**)

Christopher: These are great and important people.

Esther: (*to* **Kings**) Where are you going, earth kings?

Dawn: We are following the star. It is leading us to the Messiah, God's own son. We are from the East and have brought presents for the baby. These gifts are gold and frankincense and myrrh.

Darren: The bright and shining people said God's son was coming. The ragged, poor folk said they heard of a king. Now these rich-looking earth men are following a star.

Christopher: Can we go too? Can we go to the cowshed and see the king?

Mark: We have two more hours of resting time on earth before we continue our mission. Yes, we will go to see the king.

Mary: (*pointing to* **Space Travellers**) Look! Who are these people and what do they want.

Esther: We would like to see the king in the cowshed and worship him.

(**Space People** *go to the stage*)

(*All characters sing a carol with congregation then leave the stage area*)

THE WINTER FESTIVAL

This drama is rather like a carnival or parade, with a series of characters in turn joining the presentation. The script is interspersed with carols which are sung by the cast and audience together unless otherwise directed.

Characters: Narrator, Mary, Joseph, Angels, Shepherds, Wise Men, Lords, Ladies and Children, Minstrels, Balladeer, Postman, Workmen, Schoolchildren, Father Christmas

Costumes: All characters are appropriately costumed: biblical, medieval and contemporary

Sound effects: Trumpet fanfare (a roll on the piano may be used instead)

Props: Crib, baby doll, gifts from Wise Men, parcels for Postman, ladder for Workmen, sack for Father Christmas

The narration should be read slowly, clearly and strongly. As characters enter and take their place, the narrator should, if necessary, pause and give them time.

Narrator:
> On a wintry day, long, long ago
> A weary couple trudged through the snow,
> On their way to Bethlehem,
> As Caesar had instructed them.

(**Mary** *and* **Joseph** *enter, go to centre stage and sit*)
> They were tired as they walked around
> The cobbled streets of that ancient town,

Yet nowhere was there room to stay
Except in a stable upon the hay.

The donkeys and the cows stood by
Till in the night there came a cry,
A new babe born in the manger straw
While gazing creatures watched with awe.

(*Enter* **Angels** *and stand behind* **Mary** *and* **Joseph**)
Angels came to the starry sky
Telling the shepherds, so by and by
Those rough-coated men ran from the sheep
To peer at the baby so fast asleep.

(**Shepherds** *enter and go to the stable area*)
They told the people of the town
Of angels, and the word got round;
And later still three kings rode along
Bringing their gifts for God's own son.

(**Wise Men** *enter and go to stable*)
Baby Jesus was born that day
And his first bed was the manger hay,
Angels, shepherds, and foreign wise men
Had come there to gaze and gone home again.

CAROL—"It Came Upon a Midnight Clear"

Cold and grey this wintry night,
What celebration would make it light?
The son of God, our Jesus Christ
Brought festivity that Christmas night.

Merry minstrels, bid them come
Bring people to the banquet hall,
Christmastide has come again
Will garlands deck the walls.

Bring holly, ivy, mistletoe,
Bring burning brazier bright;
Set it here to warm our toes
And celebrate the light.

(*Trumpet fanfare*)

Herald:
Come people, lords and ladies, all,
Bring children to the festive hall

(*Enter parade of* **Lords, Ladies, Children**)

Page:
(bowing low) Milords,
We have some people here,
A travelling band of playing folk
To bring us Christmas cheer.

(*Enter* **Minstrels** *playing and singing*—"*The Holly and the Ivy*")

Narrator:
And on those olden gloomy nights
When winds were gusty and cold,
A balladeer came to the feast
And sang the songs of old.

(*Enter* **Balladeer** *and leads in singing ''Good King Wenceslas''*)

Narrator:
Yet still the years rolled on and on,
The knights were past, the dragons gone;
People made adventurous things,
Carriages with motors and planes with wings.

Still we remember year by year
The baby whose birthday is nearly here;
We added some trimmings and then some more
But celebrate still like the Christmas of yore.

Postman:
(*entering*) Merry Christmas, everyone.
Good morning to you all;
The postage cost's gone up again
But still I come to call.
Your greetings sent by post today
Reach all your loved ones far away.

Workmen:
(*entering*) Here's Christmas lights
For a busy street,
With its glittering shops
And rushing feet.
Our greetings we write with lights on high
Say 'Merry Christmas' to all who pass by.

Children:
(*entering*) Home from school
For a holiday,
It's very special
It's Christmas Day.
Someone important is coming to call
At a time when no one will see him at all.

Father Christmas:
(*entering*)
And here I am with Yuletide cheer
With reindeers and sleigh I come each year.
I have presents for all, even Mum and Dad
And all the children, whether good or bad.

Narrator:
As Christmas gathered so many things
Like partridges and snow-bound kings,
Remember in that wintry·gloom
When autumn died, and all forlorn
The people hide to fight the cold,
Still far away is springtime bold.
They look for life to light the night
So gather all for Christmas bright.
It's in the world of dark and care
That Jesus came to lighten despair,
And he comes still these wintry nights
With a smile and a promise of springtime light.

(*CAROL to be sung with congregation*)

116

FAITHFUL OLD DANIEL

Characters: Abdul, Hassim, King, Daniel, Herald, Soldiers, Servants, Narrator

Costumes: Biblical

Props: Chair (for throne), state papers. The doorway to the lions' den may be scened with a large circle or card painted to look like stone and fastened at the back of the stage in such a way that Daniel may be pushed through the door to remain hidden until it is time for him to re-emerge. It could for example be pinned to a dark brown or grey curtain, or be placed in a low 'wall' of cardboard boxes that are also painted appropriately.

Before the play begins the Narrator should rehearse the congregation in making the roar of the lions, as required in script, telling the congregation that when she reads the word 'roar' in telling the story, they should make the sound. They should rehearse the roar and then be encouraged to make the sound louder. Some children of four years and under may be frightened by the loud sound and can be warned to sit on the lap of a nearby adult so they will be less scared.

SCENE ONE

(*Enter* **Abdul** *and* **Hassim,** *looking around carefully*)

Abdul: Well, what can we do?

Hassim: He's so good, he makes me angry.

Abdul: Can't we catch him doing something wrong? He must break the law sometimes.

Hassim: He doesn't break any of our laws. That's just the problem.

(*pause*)

Abdul: I have an idea. No that wouldn't work.

Hassim: What about—No that won't do.

Abdul: I know. We will write a law that he is bound to break. There must be something he would not do. And I've got an idea of what that might be.

Hassim: What is it?

Abdul: Have you noticed how Daniel prays to his God every day? He even stands at his window where everyone can see him from the street. We must make a law that says that it is illegal to pray to his God.

Hassim: But the king would never pass a law like that, he doesn't mind Daniel's God really. We need a better idea than that!

Abdul: Maybe we should trick the king just a little bit, so he doesn't realise that Daniel will be in trouble.

Hassim: That's alright as long as he never finds out that we tricked him.

Abdul: He won't. Come on, let's get on with our plan.

(*exeunt*)

SCENE TWO

(**King** *is seated on his throne, studying some papers. Enter* **Abdul** *and* **Hassim**)

Abdul: Ahem. Ahem.

King: Yes?

Hassim: Your Majesty, we have come to make a very special request.

King: I am rather busy. You must come back later.

Abdul: We will take only a moment of your time, Your Majesty. And I do think you will like what we have to say.

Hassim: Just today we were realising how much we admire you, sir. What a brave and mighty king you are and how very much your people love you.

King: Well, yes.

Abdul: We think that you should make a law that says that for a whole month the people should worship only you.

Hassim: The people would like this law, your Majesty.

King: Are you sure they would?

Abdul: Oh yes sir. We should make the law today, before any more time passes.

King: But there may be snags to such a law. I must ask Daniel what he thinks.

Hassim: (*looking anxiously at* **Abdul**) Daniel knows what a wonderful king you are, he would be pleased with such a law.

King: You are right, of course. Daniel is such a faithful servant. Just pass me a pen and I will make the law now.

(**King** *writes on scroll, signing with a flourish. He hands the scroll to* **Hassim**.)
Give this law to the herald for announcement to the people.

(*exeunt*)

SCENE THREE

(**Herald** *enters and crosses to stage front.* **Daniel** *enters at rear of stage.*)

Herald: Hear ye! Hear ye! Today a new law has been made by the king. For one whole month all people must bow down and worship only the king; they may worship no other person and no other gods. Anyone who breaks the law will be thrown to the lions. Hear ye! Hear ye! (*exit*)

Daniel: That's strange. I wonder why the king made such a law. I am very surprised for he must realise I will worship only the one true God. I wonder if someone has tricked him into making this law.

Still I will pray to God as I always have. If someone is trying to catch me out, I will trust God to do what is best.

(**Daniel** *stands facing the audience and lifts his hands to pray.*)

(*Enter* **Soldier** *hurriedly*)

Soldier: Excuse me, sir. You are breaking the new law. It says that for a month everyone must worship King Darius and no other god!

Daniel: I can only disobey such a law. There is one god greater than King Darius, that is the God of my ancestors, of Abraham, Isaac and Jacob; he is the only God I will worship and no other.

Soldier: Then I arrest you for breaking the new law to worship the God of the Israelites and for refusing to worship King Darius. Come along with me, sir.

(*exeunt*)

SCENE FOUR

(*enter* **Abdul** *and* **Hassim**)

Abdul: We did it! Did you see, he's under arrest!

Hassim: Good. Let's get to the palace and see what happens to him. At last we may be rid of Daniel for ever.

(*exeunt*)

(*enter* **King** *and* **Servants**)

King: I can hardly believe it. I can hardly believe this has happened. Daniel must be thrown to the lions? But he is my very best minister; he is the most helpful of them all!

Servant: It's the new law that you just made. Daniel was caught worshipping the God of his ancestors.

King: I'm beginning to think I was tricked into making that law. But what can I do to save my friend Daniel. That is what I want to know, how can be be saved?

Servant: There is no way to change the law, sir. The laws of the Persians can never be changed or revoked.

King: There must be a way to save Daniel. We must think of one.

Narrator: All that day the king puzzled over the problem. How could he save Daniel? By the evening he had found no solution. Daniel would have to die.

Soldier: (*entering*) It is time to throw Daniel to the lions' den, your majesty.

King: Bring Daniel in.

(*enter two* **Soldiers** *escorting* **Daniel** *between them.*)

King: Daniel, you are to be thrown to the lions for breaking the law. I am very sorry this has happened. May your God whom you have faithfully served look after you in the lions den.

Daniel: Yes, sir.

(**Soldiers** *escort* **Daniel** *offstage, followed by* **King** *and all* **Servants**.)

Reader:

The soldiers marched down the busy street
The passing people stopped and stared.

Here was Daniel, man of God,
Being marched off by the guard.

Anxious people whispered low,
As they trod the dusty road.
Where were they taking Daniel?
Had he done something wrong?

There in the distance hear the sound,
The roar of hungry beasts. (*sound of roaring*)
Will the soldiers throw Daniel in the Lions Den?
The people watch closely to see.

The guards roll back the heavy stone
And see those lions there;
A hush falls over the waiting crowd,
As they hear lions roar. (*roar*)

Into the den Old Daniel's pushed.
The crowd cries out in fear!
And dusky silence covers the square
As the people sadly leave.

That night the King was restless and fearful. What chance had his friend Daniel got against those lions? Was it likely that the God of the Israelites could save him? And would he save him? The King tossed and turned till morning broke. Already the crowds were beginning to gather at the Lions' Den, which was unusually quiet.

(**People** *straggle onstage, looking towards the Den and down the road to see if the king is coming.*)

(*enter* **Soldiers** *and* **King**)

Soldier: Make way for his majesty the King!

King: Soldiers! Roll back the stone!

(**People** *gasp,* **Soldiers** *jump back holding weapons to protect themselves and the* **King. Daniel** *steps forward.*)

People: Hooray! Hooray! Hooray for Daniel. Long live Daniel.

King: Daniel, you are safe. How did this happen?

Daniel: Your majesty, my God sent an angel to shut the lions' mouths, because I had done no wrong.

King: I shall send a decree to all the territories and countries that I rule, that all people should honour the God of Daniel. For he is the living God whose kingdom will last for ever. He delivers and rescues, working signs and wonders in heaven and on earth. The Living God saved Daniel from the Lions!

People: Long live the God of Daniel! Hooray!

MR NOAH

A musical drama, by Maggie Durran and the UK Fisherfolk team, based on Genesis chapters 6—8.

Characters: Noah, Shem, Ham, Japheth, Neighbour 1, Neighbour 2, Neighbour 3, Narrator, Musicians and Singers. More non-speaking parts may be added, as other members of Noah's household and as other neighbours.

Props: Boat large enough for Noah and his family to stand behind: could be a large piece of card or corrugated paper, or the pulpit in the church may serve well as the ark. Tools: hammer, saw, plane, piece of wood. Percussion instruments (see music manuscript)

Costumes: None are essential, but either biblical or contemporary costume is possible.

Staging: the Narrator should be to one side of the playing area, and the musicians are preferably offstage but clearly audible.

Preparation: the music group and singers (including Noah) learn their part before the rehearsals with the whole cast.

The animal sounds, during The Incredible Ramp, are made by members of the cast and music group, see music manuscript.

Note: the congregation can participate in the rainstorm. Led by one member of the music group, the congregation follow, tapping one finger on the opposite palm, increasing to two fingers, then three as the rain increases. The leader thus controls the volume of noise and the point at which the sound stops.

The congregation may also learn the chorus of the final song before the presentation so they are able to join the final celebration.

SCENE 1. God and Mr Noah

Narrator: Once a long time ago, not long after the beginning of time, the people of the world were very wicked; not just occasionally, it was all day every day, for they had set their hearts against God. He needed to take action to deal with the situation but since the people wouldn't listen to him, he had nothing left to do but destroy everything. And he knew how to do it: he would flood the whole earth to wash away all the wickedness.

But there was one problem. There was one man who was not wicked and it wouldn't be right to wash him away. So God decided to speak to that man, whose name was Noah, and get him to build a very special sort of boat designed to float safely through even the most tremendous storms. And what was even more special about this boat was that a lot of animals would ride to safety in it, too.

Here's what happened.

(*Song: "Mr Noah"*)

Singers:

Mr Noah, do you know,
God has a job for you to do?
Mr Noah, do you know,
He wants you to build him a boat?

Noah:

Why does he want me to build him a boat?
We don't even live near the sea?
A boat will look silly in the middle of the land,
And people will laugh at me.

Singers:

Mr Noah, Do you know,
It's going to rain and rain and rain?

Mr Noah, do you know,
He's going to flood the whole earth?

Mr Noah:
I really didn't mean to disagree.
I'm ready to do what God wants.
I'd better get started right away,
There really isn't very much time.

Singers:
Mr Noah, do you know,
God wants to save the animals too?
He wants to keep them safe and sound,
So build your boat very big.

(*During narration* **Noah** *enters, crosses to boat and begins sawing and hammering; as their names are spoken his sons join him.*)

Narrator: So Noah set to work, building the boat, and he got his three sons to help him. Their names are Shem, Ham, and Japheth.

Can you imagine four men building a boat in the middle of the desert under the blazing sun? Well, they'd get very hot, wouldn't they? But there's something else. Can you imagine what the neighbours thought and what they said?

(**Neighbours** *enter and stand looking at Noah from a distance.*)

Neighbour 1: Look at him. What's he doing?

Neighbour 2: What is he doing?

Neighbour 3: That is Noah, isn't it?

Neighbour 1: What a crazy idea.

Neighbour 2: I didn't even know he had a hammer.

Neighbour 3: Hey Noah! What are you doing?

Noah: (*looking up*) Oh, hello!

Neighbour 1: What are you doing?

Neighbour 2: What are you doing up there?

Noah: I'm building a boat.

Neighbour 1: I can see it's a boat.

Neighbour 3: You're not serious are you?

Neighbour 2: This is the desert, Noah!

Noah: Let me come down and talk to you.

(**Noah** *puts down his tools; his* **sons** *also stop and watch as he crosses to talk to the* **Neighbours.** *As he approaches* **Neighbours** *talk in stage whispers.*)

Neighbour 2: What is he up to?

Neighbour 1: I think he has been out in the sun too long.

(**Noah** *reaches them*)

Neighbour 1: Why are you doing it, Noah?

Noah: God told me to.

Neighbours 2 & 3: Who?

Noah: There's going to be a flood, so I'm building a boat.

Neighbour 3: But why is it so big? Who do you think is coming with you?

Noah: Well, I'm going to take all the animals and birds, too.

(*exclamations from* **Neighbours**)

Neighbour 1: What do you mean 'all the animals and birds'?

Noah: They're coming too.

Neighbour 1: What happens if they don't want to?

Neighbour 2: Maybe God will tell them to.

Neighbour 3: Have you thought about the smell?

Neighbours 2 & 3: Phoo--eee!

Neighbour 1: Oh, come on, you lot. We're wasting our time.

(**Neighbours** *turn and go, looking back incredulously at the scene.* **Noah** *returns to his work for a short while, then he and his* **sons** *put down their tools to survey the finished ark.* **Sons** *exit*)

Noah: Hmmm... what now? ...I know—the things from the house.... Shem! Shem!

(*enter* **Shem**)

Shem: I'm here. Do you want something?

Noah: Shem, go and fetch our luggage from the house, and get the family to move in, too.

(*exit* **Shem**)
Ham!

(*enter* **Ham**)

Ham: Yes.

Noah: Will you move in the provisions from the barn?

Ham: Yes.

(*exit* **Ham**)
(*enter* **Japheth**)

Noah: Oh, and Japheth, you and I will start to move in all the animals.

Japheth: Oh, good. I've been waiting for this.

(*exeunt*)

SCENE TWO: The Incredible Ramp

Narrator: And they came by two's and more, animals, animals, and more animals.

(*Animal sounds begin*)

> Now if you've seen animals move in crowds and herds, you'll know what it was like.

(*Animal sounds fade, percussion accompaniment begins*)

> The incredible ramp of long, strong planks
> Creaked and groaned with passing feet
> Of enormous creatures like elephants,

And there's rattle and clack of echoing wood
With the clattering hooves of horses.

The air was filled with the swirling swish
Of the wings of birds in droves,
And the air was filled with chattering cackle
As each found his place to roost.

There was scratch and flurry and dash and rush
Of rodents darting by.
And the cat sat with unblinking eyes
As grey-brown rats with scurrying paws
Made for the hole in the wall.

(*slow tempo slightly*)

And the pig and the cow with indolent ease
Meandered into their stalls.

(*resume normal tempo*)

So the door was shut, the ramp hauled up,
And all were safe aboard.

SCENE THREE: When The Rain Began

(**Narrator, Noah** *and his family are onstage, the latter in the ark*)

Narrator: So the family, Noah and his sons, and all the animals waited and waited. And the neighbours waited too … and they laughed a bit, but not for long.
It was as if the whole creation was waiting to see if God would be faithful to the word he had spoken.

(*Storm begins with spots of rain, crescendo as the reading continues*)

(**Noah** *and his family look up,* **Ham** *puts out his hand*)

Ham: It's raining!

Shem: It's raining!

Japheth: It's raining!

Narrator: And the rain came.

Noah: On that day the fountain of the great deep burst forth.

Shem: And the rain fell for forty days.

Japheth: The water increased.

Noah: The ark floated.

Ham: And the waters prevailed so mightily, that all the high mountains under the whole heaven were covered.

Narrator: And the creatures of the earth died: the cattle and beasts and people. Only Noah was left.

(*storm sounds end*)

(*song: "When you've sailed away"*)

Singers:
When you've sailed away for forty days,
And the rain has fallen all the time,
You begin to wonder if you have been forgotten.
But remember, God is faithful.

(*song accompaniment played during narration*)

Narrator: And God remembered Noah was there with his family and all the animals. He caused a wind to blow on the earth, to dry up all the water.

So the water dried up, and the ark came to rest on the top of a mountain called Ararat. Noah opened the window and a raven flew out. The raven never came back.

Singers: (*repeat song: "When you've sailed away"*)

Japheth: What's happening now, Noah?

Ham: Yes, what's happening now?

Noah: Fetch me a dove, Japheth. We'll see if it can find dry land.

(**Japheth** *hands an imaginary dove to* **Noah**. Sound of **Bird**

cooing, then sound of wings as **Noah** *sends it into the air.*)

Japheth: Now we've lost a dove, too.

Ham: Oh no. It'll come back. Doves are nicer than ravens.

Shem: Here it comes.

(*Sound of wings and cooing as dove lands on* **Noah's** *outstretched hand. He hands it to* **Japheth,** *he restores it to its perch.*)

Noah: We'll try again later.

Narrator: The next time the dove flew away it came back with an olive twig in its beak. And before long the ground was dry. So God called the people out of the ark—to set free all the animals, to establish new homes in the world.

(**Noah** *and his* **family** *leave ark and go to centre stage for the final song*)

(*song: "Noah was Faithful"*)

Singers and Cast:
So there's the story of Noah
With all his animal friends,
As they were carried to safety,
When God flooded the earth.

Refrain:
Noah was faithful to God's call to him.
Noah was faithful, and God is faithful, too.

They sailed away in brand new ark
Specially built for the job.
God promised to keep them safely
And that is what he did.

Refrain

When it had rained for ages,
God dried up the water.
All the world was fresh and new,
Ready to start again.

Refrain twice with counter melody

© copyright Celebration Services (International) Ltd 1977. Used by permission.

MISTER NOAH

Maggie Durran

U.K. Fisherfolk

Chorus: G · C · D · C · D · G
Mis-ter No-ah,— do you know,— God has a job for you to do?—

C · D · G
Mis-ter No ah,— do you know,— he wants you to build him a boat?

G · Em · A7 · D7 · C · A7 · D7
Mr. Noah: Why does he want me to build him a boat? We don't ev-en live near the sea.

G · Em · A7 · D7 · A7 · D7
boat will look sil-ly in the mid-dle of the land and peo-ple will laugh at me.

G · C · D · C · D · G
Chorus: Mis-ter No ah,— do you know,— it's go-ing to rain and rain and rain?—

C · D · G
Mis-ter No-ah,— do you know,— he's go-ing to flood the whole earth?

G · Em · A7 · D7 · C · A7 · D7
Mr. Noah: I real-ly did-n't mean to dis-a-gree. I'm read-y to do what God wants I'd

G · Em · A7 · D7 · A7 · D7
bet-ter get star-ted right a-way. There real-ly is-n't ve-ry much time.

G · C · D · C · D · G
Chorus: Mis-ter No-ah,— do you know. God wants to save the an-i-mals too?— He

C · D · G
wants to keep them_ safe and sound,— so build your boat ve-ry big.

© Celebration Services (International) Ltd., 1977.
All rights reserved

THE INCREDIBLE RAMP

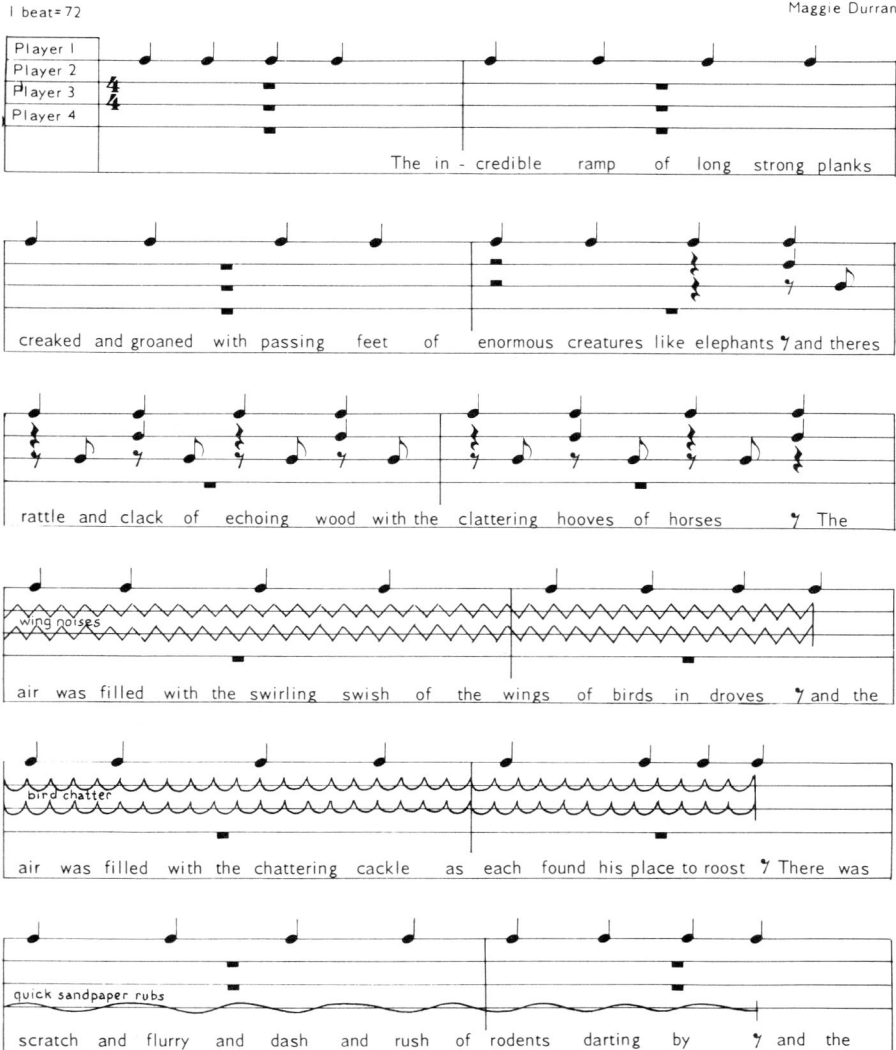

Key:

Player 1:   Main beat padded drumstick on hollow wood box or pew end etc.
Player 2:   Small drum and padded drumstick,
            also, wing noises, bird chatter and pig and cow noises.
Player 3:   Claves
            also, wing noises, bird chatter and pig and cow noises.
Player 4:   Two pieces of sand paper rubbing together,
            also, the cat's miaow and rat feet noises.

Noise instructions:

*Bird wing noises: Puff cheeks out and form lips as for whistling. Blow *hard*, place first finger horizontally *on* lips and lightly move it up and down across lips while blowing. Move at speed of flapping wings, approximately 12 per second.

*Bird chattering noises: Purse lips, place on back of fleshy part of hand between first finger and thumb, suck in (as for kissing) to make high pitched squeaking noises, keep doing so in rapid succession.

Rat feet noises: Made by tapping four fingers on edge of drum, each finger in rapid succesion; use nails to produce scratching sound.

*NB: It is desirable that player 4 also helps with these two noises for increased effect. This remains optional however.

©Celebration Services (International) Ltd., 1977. All rights reserved.

NOAH WAS FAITHFUL

Maggie Durran

U.K. Fisherfolk

No - ah was faith- ful _____ to God's call to him.

No-ah was faithful to God's call to him.   No-ah was faithful to   God's call to him.

No - ah   was faith-ful _____   and God   is faith-ful too!   too!

No-ah was faithful to God's call to him   and God   is faith-ful too!   is faithful too!

© Celebration Services (International) Ltd., 1977.
All rights reserved

Verses:

1. So, there's the sto-ry of No-ah _____ and all his an-i-mal friends

as they were car-ried to safe-ty _____ when God flood-ed the earth.

2. They sailed a-way in a brand new ark spec-ial-ly built for the job. ___ God

prom-ised to keep them safe-ly _____ and that is what ___ he did.

3. When it had rained for a-ges _____ God dried up ___ the wa-ter. ___

All the world was fresh and new, read-y to start ___ a-gain.

WHEN YOU'VE SAILED AWAY

Maggie Durran
Capo 3 (D)

Diane Davis Andrew

When you've sailed a-way for for-ty days and the rain has

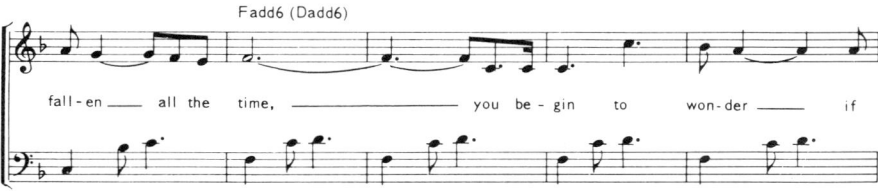

fall-en all the time, you be-gin to won-der if

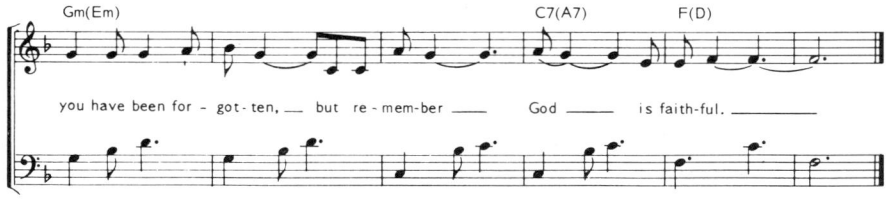

you have been for-got-ten, but re-mem-ber God is faith-ful.

Hum through tune while narrator reads. Then sing words again.

Fadd6 (Dadd6)

© Celebration Services (International) Ltd., 1977.
All rights reserved

129

CHAPTER EIGHTEEN: Workshop Preparation

The preparation for a service can occasionally be undertaken by the whole congregation, much as a family would prepare for Christmas. The outline in this chapter is for a day-long workshop, from approximately 10.00am to 3.30pm. The benefit of using a whole day, with lunch together, is that the experience of working hard and creatively together builds up friendship across the generations and encourages members to join in participatory activities they might never try otherwise. The workshop outline is built in a way that encourages and develops friendships among people who do not usually meet in church.

The workshop outline given here is general, covering a theme that considers the meaning and purpose of the Church and the Christian faith, and develops worship offerings using the gifts of the members in prayers, drama, readings and banners. For festivals such as Advent or Christmas, substitute a Christmas theme in the banner-making section, perhaps asking each group to create an illustration of one scene of the Christmas narrative. Or each group could offer a scene of Christmas as we celebrate it today with one group presenting the nativity. Choose seasonal dramas from within the book, using the classified index to help you, for the groups' preparation of readings and drama.

Careful use of linking prayers, words and songs can make these elements of a fairly eventful service into a profound act of worship. In leading the service, consider carefully how each group will find its way peacefully to the front when necessary, how links will be made and by whom. Spend more time establishing the atmosphere for worship, slightly longer in the call to worship, so to channel excitement and anticipation into the worship rather than into restlessness or anxiety.

Times are approximate. The notes in *italics* are for the benefit of the leader. Other words approximate those used to introduce the various activities to the group. With each activity is a list of the materials necessary for accomplishing the activity. Some materials appear several times during the day. See the References for sources of materials if your church does not have them already. (Some, such as scissors, may be supplied by asking everyone coming in to the workshop to bring a pair of scissors.) You may yourself wish to add other items such as bags for rubbish and cloths to wipe up spilled paint or glue.

Setting up:

Place several tables around the walls of the room and on these place the materials that will be used. Chairs are placed in rows or in a circle in preparation for the opening worship. There is no need to provide tables for people to work at as they are usually happy to spread their projects on the floor. If you expect very old people or those in wheelchairs, you *should* provide one or two tables for some work projects.

9.45 Worship and Introduction
songs
introduction to the day's activity
prayer
song

The opening worship focuses the day on worship and puts all the activity in the context of the church having gathered to prepare to worship. The group becomes conscious of its common purpose.

10.05 Partners

This activity is an icebreaker that encourages people to relax as they immediately begin to help one another. Through this and the doubling up pattern used later, every person has a new friend who helps and encourages them, whether child or adult. Wait for each age group in turn to find partners before asking the next group to choose partners.

Each person is going to have a partner for the day, someone with whom they can be friends and with whom they will work. They can share ideas and help one another.

Under 5's choose a partner first, an adult who *could be* your mum or dad.

6-11 year-olds choose an adult partner, *not* mum or dad.

All others choose a partner, not in your own family nor a close friend.

Each person here today is a child in God's family. Whether we are large or small we are still his children: no one is more or less important than anyone else to God.

What does God's child feel like today? If you were a colour what would you be? (*pause*)
If you were an animal what would you be? (*pause*)

Materials: string or wool, scissors, paper scraps of many colours

Make yourself a badge, that shows the animal you feel like, made in the colour you feel like, from the paper on the tables. Write your name on the badge and use a piece of string to hang it round your neck.

A Gift

Sit down with your partner and talk together. Find out everything you can about each other. What are your likes, dislikes, where do you go to work or school and what is it like? Where does your partner live?

Allow 10 minutes for this conversation between partners.

Materials: Large sheets of coloured paper, scissors, glue (water-based PVA), brushes, tubs of powder paint.

A large supply of relatively cheap Rainbow Paper from E J Arnold (see References for address) gives everyone opportunity to work freely. Similarly, powder paint bought from an educational suppliers such as Arnolds, can be stirred into wallpaper paste that is already mixed. This makes the paint go a long way while still producing very bright colours. Provide plastic cups for individual use with paint which is mixed in a tub, and water tubs for the used brushes to be placed in.

Now make your partner a present that will tell them that you would like them to have a good day. You could make a card or an aeroplane or a paper hat or anything else you can think of.

Allow 20 minutes for the present making.

11.00 Coffee/milk/juice time with your partner,

11.15 Gather. Each pair should join up with another to form groups of 4.

Banner making:

Materials: prepared banner backgrounds, fabric scraps which may be brought by workshop participants, scissors, water based PVA glue (see References for suppliers).

Note: The glue can easily seep through the hessian, so put newspaper under each group banner before gluing.

Before the workshop, prepare the banner backgrounds. These are large rectangles of furnishing hessian. From a local upholstery shop, purchase a length of hessian: this should be 72 inches wide and of the lightest weight, and the cheapest for its area; this will be cut into pieces 36 inches by 27 inches—so on an estimate of the numbers of people you will have at your workshop calculate the amount you should buy. Cut the hessian into pieces of the stated size. Cut out circles of 5 inch diameter (13 cm) from felt or other non-fraying fabric, for wheels. Cut two of these wheels for each banner. Cut strips, one for each group banner background, 1 inch by 26 inches (2.5 cm by 66 cm). Glue two wheels and one strip (base of carriage) to each background, across the 27 inch side, which becomes the bottom of the picture. Use water-based PVA glue or fabric glue.

Each group is going to make a piece of a large banner. When all the pieces are put together the workshop participants will have a picture that illustrates the life of the church.

It is important that each member of the groups listen to all the other members of that group. Hear everyone's thoughts and opinions; no one can know someone else's thoughts without first listening.

Each group should talk together about what the Church is for. What has God called this church to be? What is this church especially good at doing? What is its mission? What does each group member think the church should be doing more of? One person in your group may take notes of everyone's ideas and as a group allow time for everyone's ideas and opinions. Don't criticise or ignore the contributions of other group members.

Think of a way to represent your group's ideas on the banner. Do not use words, make your banner a picture. On group banner background you will find there is already the wheels and chassis for a train carriage, one group banner will represent the engine. When all the groups have finished the larger banner will show the church as a train that is travelling along; its pictures illustrating the work and worship of the church.

As each group finishes its banner hang them consecutively behind the engine, along one wall of the church building.

Allow 60 minutes for this activity, with 15 minutes for clearing up before lunch.

12.30 Lunch together.
1.30 Gather together in the same groups as the morning.

Prayers

Materials: local and national newspapers, church newsletters, glue, scissors, felt pens, large sheets of paper, Blutak.

Each four should collect a couple of local newspapers and a few church newsletters.

Look through the newsletters and papers and find the following:

Prayers that have been answered. Maybe your church has been praying for someone who is now better. You may have prayed for money and some has been given. Cut out these items.

Prayer requests. What is your church still praying for? In the newspaper what concerns are there that your church has prayed for, for example, people in Ethiopia. Cut out these items.

Your prayers. Find items that each of you would like to pray for because they are relevant to you. Maybe they refer to a neighbour of yours, someone in your factory, someone at school or someone who has the same handicap as someone in your family, so you understand. Cut out these items.

Collect a large sheet of paper and paste your group's cuttings onto it.

Under each cutting you should write what you would like to say to God. You may want to grumble a little bit. You may want to say thank you. You may want to ask him to do something. You may ask him what you can do.

When we work on prayers together this way, no one person in the church is trying to say prayers for everyone or trying to make a presentation of their prayers. We can all recognise these prayer concerns and present them in many different ways.

Listen to everyone in your group and don't spend time trying to get others to say their prayers your way. God is good at understanding all sorts and is not offended about different ways of saying things.

When you have finished, fix your paper to the wall with some Blutak: the groups will be able to see the prayers of everyone present.

Allow 45 minutes for this activity

2.30 Break for drinks with your partner.

A Service

Rejoin the four you had this morning. Then double up with another group of four to become **groups of eight**.

Each group is given a task from the following list.

1. Make a puppet play of a New Testament story using the script for "The Five Thousand" on page 52.

2. Prepare one of the following dances as a group: "On Tiptoe", "Come go with me to that land", or "God is our Father".

3. Write a psalm from everyone. Go to all the other groups and ask them for things that they'd like to say to God, grumbles, thanks, praise. Put these together to make a psalm which is on large sheets of paper so the whole groups (and church) can all read it aloud together.

4. Make a play from a Bible story, using the script for "The Walls Came Tumbling Down" on page 40

5. Prepare a play on a parable of a contemporary theme, for the sermon. Use either "Once upon a Compost Heap", "Time to Wake Up", or "The Third Little Piggy".

6. Using coloured paper as a background, (an alternative would be to use banner backing) each group is to make a pictorial representation of a phrase of the Lord's prayer. Use no words.

   phrases:

   Our Father in heaven, hallowed be your name.

   Your kingdom come, your will be done on earth as in heaven.

   Give us this day our daily bread,

   Forgive us our sins as we forgive those who sin against us.

   Lead us not into temptation but deliver us from evil.

   For thine is the kingdom the power and the glory, for ever.

7. Take the opening prayer from the **Alternative Service Book** and illustrate the phrases on hessian backgrounds. These are mounted on lengths of dowelling or bamboo and carried as processional banners at the beginning of the worship. They are then displayed for the reading of the prayer which on this occasion might be said by all present:

We have come together as the family of God in our Father's presence
to offer him praise and thanksgiving,
to hear and receive his holy word,
to bring before him the needs of the world,
to ask his forgiveness of our sins,
and to seek his grace,
that through his son Jesus Christ we may give ourselves to his service.

Materials: Look carefully at each drama and reading script and collect the necessary props and costumes. In addition collect white paper and large felt pens for the psalm writers, coloured paper, scissors, glue for the illustrators of the Lord's Prayer, or banner materials for the processional banners. A source of music will be necessary for the group that is dancing: either use a cassette recorder with the song chosen or ask a guitarist to join this group—making a nine-member group.

During the remainder of the workshop groups will prepare items for presentation during the worship service, fitting the theme of the church's life and mission. The suggestions cater for a large number of workshop participants—you may have less so select activities appropriate to your members and your service.

Allow 60 minutes for these activities time with 15 minutes for clearing up.

3.30 *Finish the session. Round up the workshop with a time together. Recollect with everyone what they have done today. Point out the many visual items on the walls. Explain how other items will be included in the service in church, the following day. Ask each person to think of what they have most enjoyed about the day. Give opportunity for individuals to say this to all those present. What have participants enjoyed most about their partner and working together? They can tell their partners. What have the workshop participants learned today? They can tell the whole workshop group. Gather these contributions in a closing prayer of thanks and praise. As appropriate, have a final song and close by saying The Grace together.*

References and Reading List

The Child in the Church. British Council of Churches, 1976.

Faith in the City. Report of the Archbishop of Canterbury's Commission on Urban Priority Areas, 1985.

Hymns Ancient and Modern Revised. 1981.

Understanding Christian Nurture. British Council of Churches, 1981.

Apostolos-Cappadona, Diane (Ed), *The Sacred Play of Children*. Seabury, 1983.

Baumohl, Anton, *Making Adult Disciples*. Scripture Union, 1984.

Buchanan, Colin (Ed), *Nurturing Children in Communion*. Grove Liturgical Study, 1985.

Durran, Maggie and Nobbs, Val, *Festive Seasons*. Marshall Pickering, 1987.

Durran, Maggie, *Hello, I'm a Person Too*. Celebration, 1984.

Durran, Maggie, *Understanding Children*. Marshall Pickering, 1987.

Egler, Larry and Fijan, Carol, *Making Puppets Come Alive*. David and Charles, 1973.

Friere, Paulo, *Pedagogy of the Oppressed*. Seabury, 1974.

Holeton, David, *Infant Communion — Then and Now*. Grove Liturgical Study No 27, 1981.

Kellmer, Pringle Mia, *The Needs of Children*. Hutchinson, 1980.

Kennedy, Neville Gwen and Westhof, John H III, *Learning Through Liturgy*. Seabury, 1978.

Keys Barker, Martha and the Fisherfolk, *Building Worship Together*. Celebration, 1981.

Moltmann, Jurgen, *The Power of the Powerless*. SCM Press, 1983.

The Offchurch Group, *All Generations*. CIO, 1980.

Pulkingham, Betty and Farra, Mimi, *Cry Hosanna*. Hodder and Stoughton, 1980.

Pulkingham, Betty and Harper, Jeanne, *Fresh Sounds*. Hodder and Stoughton, 1976.

Pulkingham, Betty and Harper, Jeanne, *Sound of Living Waters*. Hodder and Stoughton, 1974.

Sutcliffe, John M, *Learning Community*. Denholm House Press, 1974.

Tiller, John, *A Strategy fot the Church's Ministry*. CIO, 1985.

Weber, Hans-Ruedi, *Jesus and the Children*. World Council of Churches, 1979.

Weil, Louis, *Sacraments and Liturgy*. Basil Blackwell, 1973.

Westerhof, John H III, *Bringing up Children in the Christian Faith*. Winston Press, 1980.

Westerhof, John H III, *Will Our Children Have Faith?* Seabury, 1976.

Whitaker, E C, *The Baptismal Liturgy*. SPCK, 1981.

For booklets that contain folk dances contact: English Folk Dance and Song Society, Cecil Sharpe House, 2 Regents Park Road, London, NW1.

For craft materials, try E.J. Arnold, Parkside Lane, Drewsbury Road, Leeds, LS11 5TD.

For Bible Puppet Kits write to Celebration, 58 High Street, Bletchingley, Surrey, RH1 4PA.

Index of Scripts

	chapter	type	season
Bread from Heaven	8	R	a
By the Sea	6	D	a
Christmas Space Travellers	17	D	C
Come Go with me to that Land	10	DA	a
Crossing the Red Sea	6	D/C	a
The Egg and the Chick	8	D	E
Expectations	8	R	C
Faithful Old Daniel	17	D	a
The Five Thousand	7	N/P	a
Glory	8	R	a
God is Our Father	10	DA	a
The Good Samaritan	7	N/P	a
Horses and Chariots of Fire	6	D/C	a
The Jordan Bank	6	D	a
King Hezekiah	5	R/C	a
The Light of the World	8	R	a
The Most Precious Pearl	8	N/M	a
Mr Noah	17	D/MU	a
The Mustard Tree that Grew	8	D	a
Old Dry Bones	5	R	a
Once Upon a Compost Heap	8	N/M	a
On Tiptoe	10	DA	a
Parable of the Lamp	3	N/M	a
Ruth and Naomi	5	R	a
The Storm at Sea	6	D/C	a
The Third Little Piggy	8	D	a
Through the Desert	6	D/C	a
Time to Wake Up	8	N/M	C
To David's Town	7	N/P or C/D	C
Treasures	6	N/M	a
The Walls Came Tumbling Down	6	N/M or P	a
Whom Shall I Send?	5	R	a
The Winter Festival	17	D	C
Wise and Foolish Maidens	6	N/M	a
Winter Psalm	5	R/M and C	a

Key:

DA	Dance
D	Drama
N	Narration
M	Mime
MU	Musical
C	Congregational
R	Reading
P	Puppets
a	Any
C	Christmas
E	Easter